KANSAI
COOL

For my parents

KANSAI COOL

A Journey into the Cultural Heartland of Japan

CHRISTAL WHELAN

TUTTLE Publishing

Tokyo | Rutland, Vermont | Singapore

Published by Tuttle Publishing, an imprint of Periplus Editions (HK) Ltd.

www.tuttlepublishing.com

Copyright © 2014 by Christal Whelan

Library of Congress Cataloging-in-Publication Data for this title is in progress

ISBN 978- 4-8053-1280-3

Exact or adapted versions of chapters 2-9 and 11-13 first appeared in *The Daily Yomiuri column Kansai Culturescapes* between January 2011 and April 2012.

Distributed by

North America, Latin America & Europe
Tuttle Publishing
364 Innovation Drive
North Clarendon,
VT 05759-9436 U.S.A.
Tel: 1 (802) 773-8930
Fax: 1 (802) 773-6993
info@tuttlepublishing.com
www.tuttlepublishing.com

Japan
Tuttle Publishing
Yaekari Building 3rd Floor
5-4-12 Osaki, Shinagawa-ku
Tokyo 1410032, Japan
Tel: (81) 3 5437 0171
Fax: (81) 3 5437 0755
sales@tuttle.co.jp
www.tuttle.co.jp

Asia Pacific
Berkeley Books Pte. Ltd.
61 Tai Seng Avenue #02-12,
Singapore 534167
Tel: (65) 6280-1330
Fax: (65) 6280-6290
inquiries@periplus.com.sg
www.periplus.com

First edition
17 16 15 14   10 9 8 7 6 5 4 3 2 1   1312MP

Printed in Singapore

Contents

PART IV: THE ARTS

PART V: YOUTH CULTURE

PART VI: RELIGION

Acknowledgements

I HAD A GREAT DEAL of help the whole way in making this book. My thanks first to the Japanese people who gave so generously of their time and knowledge while I engaged in my perpetual scouting missions across Kansai in order to research the subjects included in this book. My various forays into Japan's religious traditions actually date back two decades. Eiheiji, Koyasan, Tsubaki Grand Shrine, Hagurosan, are just a few of the places where I spent time in retreats of varying duration. Each one has added a rich dimension to my life for which I am deeply grateful.

I would like to extend my thanks to *The Daily Yomiuri (The Japan News)*, for whom I worked as a columnist writing "Kansai Culturescapes" from my base in Kyoto from 2011-2012, and for their permission to include those essays among the new ones in the present collection. I am especially indebted to my chief editors Yumiko Miyai and Kakuya Ishida. Thank you also, Mr. Yoshihiro Kaida of the Kyoto International Cultural Association, for permission to reprint the essay "Gratitude." It's the welcome mat of the whole collection.

My esteem for Tuttle Publishing remains as strong as ever for their enduring dedication to making Japan better known to the world. I am thankful to my masterful editor, Terri Jadick, for shepherding this book to the finish in a timely and thorough manner. In the U.S., I enjoyed my affiliation with the East Asian Studies Program at the Johns Hopkins University. Program Director, Joel Andreas, welcomed me on board and granted me access to the excellent libraries and participation in seminars.

A hearty thanks to others, mostly in Japan—to Christopher Fryman for his generosity and liaising expertise, and to all the contributing photographers: John Einarsen, Hiroshi Mimura, Moho, Kazuhiko Susukida, Daniel Peralta, and to Ittoen for allowing me to reprint one of their photos, and to Nariko Yamashita of TOTO Ltd. who granted me to use of photos from the company's collection. Thanks also to Yu Tsukinaga who allowed her lovely watercolor to be reproduced here.

I remain grateful for the strong support and early influence of Takie Sugiyama Lebra,. To Donald Richie and Donald Keene—the "grandfathers" of Japanese studies whose inspiration embraced a whole generation—thank you both for being such superb models.

This book would not exist at all were it not for two other people. Therefore, I dedicate this book to my mother and father for their sustained belief in me. My gratitude for their support is incalculable.

Introduction
West of the Toll Gate

JAPAN IS EXCEEDINGLY MOUNTAINOUS, and long from north to south, and for most of its history has been defined more by region than by nation. A quick look at a nautical map heightens the impression that aside from the four main islands the Japanese archipelago is actually made up of more than three thousand smaller islands with over half the landmass covered by forests. Besides these natural barriers of sea and mountain, for much of the country's history poor transportation also hindered communication among the various regions. Over time, this insularity fostered a robust regional diversity that remains a vibrant feature of the country even today.

Though Japan has eight regions, this collection of short essays is about only one of them—Kansai—located in the southern-central part of Honshu, Japan's big middle island. Within this expanse lie seven prefectures equivalent to states or provinces: Kyoto, Nara, Osaka, Hyogo, Shiga, Wakayama, and Mie (1). Roughly nineteen percent of the country's 127,000 inhabitants reside here. During spring and fall, the numbers swell temporarily as Japanese from all over the country descend on the region to witness the ritual of falling cherry blossoms or the warm spectrum of autumn colors and reconnect to a collective cultural reservoir. After all, Kansai is immensely attractive for its historical depth and because it is the font of much of what is considered quintessentially Japanese by people both inside and outside the country—the tea ceremony, the art of flower arrangement, the performing arts of kabuki, noh, and joruri puppet theater, traditional cuisine, prominent literary works such as *The Pillow Book and The Tale of Genji* (both written by women), shrine and temple architecture, ancient pilgrimage routes, and the hub of an astonishing variety of Buddhism.

The ancient capitals of Japan—Osaka, Nara, and Kyoto—are all cities that are located in the heartland of Kansai (also called Kinki). In terms of early exchanges with Asia, the Seto Inland Sea, a waterway that separates Honshu from Shikoku island, has served as the great gateway to Japan where ideas and material objects spread from the port of Naniwazu (Osaka) throughout Kansai. From this region, influences radiated outward leaving no part of the country untouched. Nara, the country's first permanent capital, is also home to the world's oldest wooden structure—Horyuji temple—a fitting tribute to the city (where deer roam freely) that marked the last stop in the easternmost route of the Silk Road.

The term "Kansai" first emerged during the Heian period (794-1185) as a practical way to distinguish the political and cultural center of the country at that time—basically Nara and Kyoto—from the increasing development of the territory around Japan's largest plain located in eastern Honshu—the Kanto. Kansai means "west of the tollgate," and referred to lands in the western central part of Honshu. The *tollgate* in its name denotes one of the ancient border stations established as early as the 10th century. On the other side of the check point at Otsu in Shiga prefecture lay the region of Kanto meaning "east of the tollgate." Although the seat of political and economic power has shifted multiple times throughout Japan's history, Kanto and Kansai have come to represent two distinct cultural and linguistic areas today. In a country where regionalism remains strong, the two stand as shorthand for an internal east-west divide roughly translated as Tokyo and Osaka—the two main economic powerhouses of the nation and the most populous metropolises of Japan.

The characterization of the two regions as much more than geographical entities began to develop in earnest during the

Kamakura period (1185-1333) with the burgeoning of a samurai class that spread throughout the center of Honshu in a bid for supremacy. Warriors of the two most powerful clans—the Minamoto and the Taira—struggled and ultimately the Minanmoto gained ascendancy, a victory that precipitated the emperor with the Taira to flee back to western Japan. By 1192, the Minamoto clan's victory at the Battle of Dan-no-Ura signaled the definitive rise of the Minamoto clan with Minamoto-no-Yoritomo at its head and Japan's first shogun or Military Commander. The golden age of the Heian era with its nobles and courtly pastimes had begun to fade and a powerful new military orientation with the Kamakura shogunate stood in its stead. Although the capital remained in Kyoto many functions of the government were actually transferred to Kamakura in the Kanto region some 32 miles southwest of Tokyo.

The bifurcation of power divided between the emperor and the shogun and the association of each with distinct regions forms the basis of an enduring Kansai-Kanto rivalry. The symbolic and cultural power of the emperor came to be associated with the Kansai and the political and military power of the state embodied by the shogun with Kanto. Both the Kamakura shogunate and later the Tokugawa were both based in Kanto. But it was during the Tokugawa era that the distinctions between Kansai and Kanto developed with the features recognizable today. In 1603, by dint of his victory at the Battle of Sekigahara, Tokugawa Ieyasu managed to unify a country then composed of small warring states and to establish the seat of his governmen in Edo (now Tokyo). The next 265 years came to be known as the Edo period (1603-1868) a time of extraordinary economic and cultural development for Japan in which a vibrant merchant class arose alongside the samurai. However, to protect itself from divisive foreign influences, the country adopted a policy of isolation and closed itself to the world with virtually no exchanges. Self-sufficient in all its resources, Japan remained peaceful, productive, and stable during the Edo period. The shogun controlled about one forth of the country, including Kansai.

A unique feature of the Tokugawa shogunate was the practice by which samurai, as part of their service to their feudal lord or *daimyo*, resided in Edo in alternating years and offered their services there. Huge retinues of samurai lived in this bustling city at any given time though life there was hugely expensive for them. In the early eighteenth century, Edo was the largest city in the world with an estimated population of 1 to 1.25 million. The traffic back and forth alone from home fief to Edo required a system of post-stations where the samurai could rest along their journey. Merchants set up shops, lodgings, and stores around the many post-stations along the routes. In addition to commuting samurai, travel boomed among the common people who sought spiritual refreshment through pilgrimages. The Ise shrine in Mie, Japan's most revered Shinto complex, became a favorite destination for pilgrims.

During the Edo period Osaka developed into a great commercial center. With the construction of a canal, merchants could easily transport goods along the whole coast of the Sea of Japan. In addition, a series of *kurayashiki*, warehouses that served also as sales offices, were built there for various fiefs. Controlled by the shogunate, they gave special privileges to the wholesale dealers and brokers who managed them. The prototype of the Kansai merchant was Takatoshi Mitsui, son of a sake brewer from Mie. The Mitsui family grew to be the largest merchant house of the Tokugawa period and the richest family in Japan. In the late seventeenth century the Mitsuis became the officially chartered merchants for the Tokugawa shogunate.

They opened shops and a department store along a main street in Edo (that later became Mitsukoshi). They were among the first to advertise in Japan by giving away free umbrellas to shoppers in their stores. When it rained, the Mitsui logo could be seen all over the capital. They introduced methods of commerce by means of money when the use of money in trading was virtually unknown. They set up money changing shops in Osaka to convert taxes that were paid in rice into money and even handled the dangerous transfer of funds from Osaka to Edo.

In the mid-nineteenth century Japan ended its long self-imposed seclusion from the rest of the world by reopening its ports and negotiating treaties with the U.S. and certain European nations. As part of a series of reforms initiated by the new and modernizing Meiji government, the capital was transferred once again, but this time out of the Kansai region altogether, and to its present location in Tokyo. This relocation also symbolized the shift from a feudal to a modern society that had required significant revolutionary and visionary forces to topple the shogun, dismantle the powerful and entrenched feudal system, and restore the emperor as head of state. Until this time, the emperor and nobles had always resided in Kansai.

But now the Imperial Palace in Kyoto lay empty. In the 1870s the new government turned its attention to reorganizing the country from a multitude of fiefdoms into forty-seven newly configured administrative territories or prefectures.

Within the new order, Osaka maintained its prestige as a thriving city of commerce that had served as the major supplier of goods to the city of Edo. However, long after this period had passed, the association of samurai with Tokyo (Kanto) and merchants with Osaka (Kansai) became a standard cultural image. In fact, I had read about a typical greeting in Osaka that I was eager to hear: *Mookkarimakka?* ("Are you making money?"). Fortunately, no one ever greeted me with this salutation. It seems to have disappeared altogether now except perhaps when used as a joke as suggested by DC Palter and Kaoru Slotsve in their book *Colloquial Kansai Japanese.*

The use of different dialects continues to distinguish the two contrasting regions but with one enormous difference. Once the capital was established in Tokyo, the new government selected an uptown variant of Tokyo dialect as the language to be taught as standard "Japanese" in schools across the country. This is the same language foreigners study when they learn "Japanese" in their own schools and universities. Given the centralization of power today in Tokyo the use of this standard language by broadcasters on NHK national television, Japanese people everywhere have acquired fluency in this officially sanctioned version of Japanese. Nevertheless, people in Kansai are not only proud of their heritage but simply more comfortable using their own dialects in daily conversation.

To spend even a little time in Kyoto or Osaka, is to develop an ear for the cadence and unique vocabulary of *Kansai-ben* or western dialect that actually consist of many sub-dialects. The first thing that stands out is the ubiquitous sound of "wa" at the end of sentences. This word has no meaning in itself beyond adding emphasis to whatever the speaker is saying. In Kansai both men and women use it frequently. Tokyoites, on the other hand, use the same "wa" at the end of a sentence for emphasis though enunciating it more softly. But in this case, it is an exclusive feature of women's speech.

As a rule, Kansai dialect is much more melodic because speakers tend to accentuate the first syllable of words while Kanto speech is generally flatter. Kansai natives also often repeat the same word twice as in the commonly heard: *Kamahen, kamahen* ("I don't mind.") as my landlady often said to me to convey empathy. Another striking difference is how the "s" sound in standard Japanese often becomes an "h" in Kansai. Hence, "Mr. Tanaka" or "Ms. Tanaka" is *Tanaka-han* in Kansai, and *Tanaka-san* in Tokyo. Verb endings are also different. Endings in *–haru* and negative *-hen* contrast with the *–ru* and *-nai*. Some vocabulary is simply different such as the word for "chicken meat": *kashiwa* in Kansai and *tori-niku* in most other places. People in Kansai use *okini* to say "thank you" while *arigatoo* is the standard phrase in Japanese. Finally, to say "please" when asking for a favor— *onegai shimasu* (a phrase used constantly in Japan) becomes *tanomu wa* in Kansai.

Standardized education, national media, and the mobility of people especially moving from rural to urban areas has undeniably weakened dialects, but for the most part I found Kansai-ben still quite robust in Kyoto and parts of Osaka. Only once, when conversing with a man from Yao [southeastern Osaka] did I find myself drifting in and out of comprehension. The interest in regional and prefectural differences in Japan seems to wax and wane as well. In recent years, several books have been written that explore the country's internal diversity. Referred to as *kenminsei*, or "prefectural personality", these works describe the typical behaviors that each prefecture inculcates in the people born and raised in an area with a common history, geography, and environmental conditions.

Anthropologist Takao Sofue was among the first to specialize in the subject as early as the 1970s. Koichi Otani later wrote about the personality of Osakans, referring to his subject as "Osakalogy". Most recently, marketing consultant Shinichi Yano has promoted prefectural personality as a way to devise sales strategies for various regions and even authored a book for a niche market on the prefectural personalities of Japanese women. Yomiuri TV launched a popular television program in 2007 "Himitsu no Kenmin Show" in which the hosts invite celebrities on the show to represent their own prefecture. After a discussion of the unique features and customs, the celebrity travels live to the prefecture to interview people in what may sometimes turn into a comical attempt to justify the earlier claims.

A common example of a Kansai-Kanto contrast concerns escalator etiquette. In Kansai people typically stand to the right and walkers pass on the left side. In Kanto, on the other hand, everyone stands on the left and walkers pass by on the right. The reason often given (if any) for this predictable set of behaviors is a historical one. Because Tokyo was a city of samurai, even now contemporary people prefer to stay on the left in order to easily draw their swords traditionally kept on the right side. As Osaka was a town of merchants, they still prefer the right side for the protection it offers since traditionally they carried their belongings in the right hand. In any case, one outcome of the current revival of interest in regional or prefectural character has been to raise awareness in Japan of the internal diversity of the country. It also makes it difficult for non-Japanese to speak glibly about the national character of the Japanese when there is actually so much regional and local diversity.

With Kyoto and Nara as the political and cultural center of Japan since the beginning of recorded history, and Shiga, Kobe, and Osaka the great commercial centers during the Edo period, Kansai possesses a complex cultural identity. Even within Kansai itself each prefecture is known for its distinctive character. Kansai people not from Kyoto often describe Kyotoites as "aloof" or "two-faced" since they value reserve and do not easily reveal directly what is on their minds, while Osakans are often called the "Latins of Japan" for being warm, down-to-earth, outgoing, and funny. It was here that Manzai originated—the stand-up comedian duos of the straight man and the funny man. Although both Kyoto and Osaka are known for their delicate cuisine, when compared to each other, the emphais of Kyoto easily shifts to fashion as the saying demonstrates: *Kyo no kidaore, Osaka no Kuidaore* (Kyoto people ruin themselves for clothing, and people of Osaka on food). People from Shiga, known for their business savvy, have long cultivated a philosophy of *sanpo-yoshi* or "three-way satis-faction" in which buyer, seller, and the society at large should all be beneficiaries of any economic transaction for it to be consid-ered a success. From the region have come the founders of such notable companies as the trading giant Marubeni and Wacoal, the famed producer of lingerie.

Sometimes the contrast between Kansai and Kanto is cast as historical pique since Kyoto lost its status as the nation's capital in the nineteenth century. Nevertheless, Kyoto not only maintains a prestige as the birthplace of Japanese culture but is also fre-quently charged as the keeper of Japan's traditions in the present while Tokyo gets regularly blamed for all forms of standardization. While this often smacks of mere caricature, it is intriguing how the distinction between Kansai and Kanto was sufficiently intact as to influence foreign policy during the Allied fire bombings in World War II. While bombs devastated a great deal of Sakai and Osaka, Kyoto, the country's capital for over a thousand years, was spared because of its cultural and historical significance. Tokyo hardly received such consideration and was not spared from heavy bombing. As a result, Kyoto was able to continue to take pride in its visible heritage of ancient temples and castles while Tokyo lost most of its own. Japan's modern capital had no choice but to rebuild and modernize. Therefore, much of Tokyo is comparatively new, having been built within just the last six and half decades.

In writing this book I wanted to return to an earlier time when I first set foot in Japan and experienced everything as strangely new. Full of questions but with few ready answers, my enthusiasm carried me in multiple directions at once. At that time, I could have benefited from a guidebook, not one chock-a-block with historical personages and dates too easily forgotten (for such books exist aplenty), but one that would have served more as a cultural compass to allow me to discover patterns and trends and help me find my own way. This book is intended to be just that kind of guide, the one I didn't have, to assist those who desire to go beyond the cultural stereotypes, predictable tourist sites, and would appreciate a combination of contemporary focus with more interpretive depth while traveling through a vibrant and ever-evolving region. This book is also intended for the many Japanese I have known over the years who for one reason or another expressed regret that they had scant opportunity to explore their own country. I have heard this complaint again and again from Japanese at home and abroad and attempt to respond to it with this book.

My own interest in Japan began as a fascination with the country's first contact with the West vis-à-vis the arrival of Portuguese and Spanish Jesuits and Franciscans in the sixteenth and seventeenth centuries. I wondered why a mutually engaging relationship that had lasted a century then deteriorated and precipitated the country into a long era devoid of all international exchanges save but a small community of Dutch and Chinese on a tiny island in Nagasaki built for this sole purpose. The launching point of my interest gradually expanded to encompass an ever broader cultural interest in Japan that sustained me throughout my professional training as an anthropologist. Over the years I have heard many diverse interpretations and characterizations of the country from sociologists, anthropologists, visitors, expats, novelists, psychoanalysts, and policymakers that in their totality conjure up the South Asian parable of the blind men and the elephant.

Asked to determine what an elephant looks like by touching it, each man feeling a single part of the animal—tail, trunk, tusk, leg, ear, and belly—describes the elephant as a very different kind of creature. In the same way, we can read that Japan is a "compact culture" (O-Young Lee), a "dependency culture" (Takeo Doi), a "shame culture" (Ruth Benedict), a "vertical society" (Chie Nakane), a "typhoon mentality" (Edwin Reischauer), a "wrapping culture" (Joy Hendry), a "kimono mind" (Bernard Rudofsky), a "culture of humiliation" (Amélie Nothomb), and the most recent descriptor a "cool culture," (METI). The actual expression the Ministry of Economy Trade and Industry uses is "Cool Japan" to describe a country in which popular culture has now come to signify the whole in the new geopolitics of soft power officially promoted by the Japanese government today with its ambassadors of cool.

Though I am indebted to all of those mentioned above for teaching me about some aspect of Japan, and to countless others less conducive to sound bytes, I am uncomfortable with master concepts and summations that attempt to capture the main spring of any culture or civilization. However, there are two words that express approaches to life that I have found pervasive throughout Japan. They are: *gambaru/gambatte*, and *kansha. Gambaru* can mean "keep trying" or "go for it." It exhorts a person to make the most sincere effort possible in any undertaking. It also implies that the outcome is far less important than the effort put into something. Ivan Morris captured the sentiment well in his elegant book—*The Nobility of Failure: Tragic Heroes in the History of*

Japan—that tells the stories of various heroes who failed to attain their goals, and often losing their lives in the process. Not victorious in any simplistic way, yet in Japan they are nonetheless considered heroes. What they possessed was a spirit of *gambaru* as they threw everything they had into their effort. The word *kansha* translates as "gratitude" and is an orientation that recognizes that a person never accomplishes anything alone but rather is supported throughout life by innumerable people, the natural world, and organizations. The opposite of any notion of self-reliance, it goes a long way in keeping the ego in check.

For the most part, I have attempted through description to avoid grasping another part of the elephant myself. That said, I have allowed a few principles to guide my approach. The overarching theme of all these chapters is cultural change and the incessant tug-of-war between preservation and innovation. I found this issue particularly acute in Kyoto, the heartland of Japanese tradition where *maiko*, apprentices to full-fledged geisha, can still be seen stepping from limousines in the Gion district and shuffling to their appointments in steep platform willow-wood *pokkuri* thongs, while Buddhist monks in straw sandals and broad conical hats that double as umbrellas roam the back streets of the city chanting with begging-bowls in hand and eat only what they receive in alms.

To some extent, the issues raised in these chapters can hardly be confined to the Kansai region alone and are applicable throughout the country. But given the depth of tradition in the Kansai, loss of this same tradition and adaptive innovation strike a particularly poignant note. After all, the roots go deeper and traditions tend to hang on longer here. In addition, these were the specific cases that faced me in my daily environs in Kyoto and are not meant to be exhaustive or to carry the last word. Whenever possible, I compare the Japanese situation to a comparable one outside the country in order to mitigate the tendency to single out Japan as an exception within the world or even within the Asian sphere.

Though I do not deal specifically in this book with the efforts to preserve the traditional houses or *machiya*, counterparts to that situation exist elsewhere—Germany's struggle to save the half-timbered houses of Quedinburg from oblivion or Bai Shi-yuan's decades-long crusade in China to save the merchant houses of Huizhou from demolition. My point in making such comparisons is not to trivialize the immediacy of the issue in Japan but rather to open up more space in which to consider the problem and also to prevent a revival of the *nihonjinron* or "Japanese uniqueness" theories popular intermittently from the 60s through the 1980s. Sometimes I also wish to show the multiple streams of influence, including the intersection between local and global, which have gone into making what we often consider as something distinctly "Japanese" in art or industry.

The more artists and artisans I came to know in Kyoto and Osaka convinced me that they approach their own work in ways that are never static. Yasushi Noguchi, for example, a master craftsman who produces the gold and silver threads used in brocaded *obi* weaving, spoke of the waning *obi* industry in the Nishijin district of Kyoto but not in the spirit of a lone dinosaur watching his world disappear around him. Hardly a Luddite, he spoke refreshingly and pragmatically about the situation with which he had wrestled constantly in order to come up with a creative solution.

While Western observers often lament the incursions of modernity into traditional spheres in Japan (and may well romanticize the past), this master craftsman who certainly has much more at stake did not appear to be in the grip of nostalgia. The resilience and flexibility his position represented is what I came to cherish most in the Kansai. I caught a glimpse of it when Noguchi showed me some of his abstract artwork using the same gold and silver leaf on canvas that he also used to roll around the threads for weaving the *obi*. Engaged with the times, Noguchi had diversified and remained superbly creative in two different spheres. There will probably always be a need to produce *obi* but not in the quantities of previous eras when the kimono was the daily wear of every Japanese. To preserve continuity amidst the demands of change requires openness and creative response.

This book owes much to *The Daily Yomiuri (*which reinvented itself as *The Japan News* in April 2013), an English-language national newspaper, for which I wrote a column "Kansai Culturescapes" between 2011-2012. My task was to choose a subject and write about Kansai through an "anthropological lens." Since the column appeared monthly as a full page in the Sunday travel section, it was imperative that I move beyond commentary and introduce readers to actual places they could visit while showing them photos to further entice them to travel. Because many of the newspaper's readers are expats who would be bored by places a first-time visitor might enjoy, I sought to introduce venues that would surprise even these old "Japan hands" well versed in the customs and peculiarities of Japan.

Fortunately, I happened to be living in the eastern hills of Kyoto then, just off the Philosopher's Path, five minutes from one of the greatest temples in Japan—Ginkakuji (Silver Pavilion). The window to my second-floor dwelling faced a small lane up which tourists passed daily to reach several distinguished temples, shrines, and mausoleums further up the hill. As they trundled by in organized tours, motley bands of friends, or couples, I grew accustomed to overhearing snippets of their conversations in dozens of languages of the world, only some of which I understood. The comments were often as instructive as they were entertaining. "Oh no, not another temple!" I once heard a female voice whine below and peeked out my window to see a young woman facing her family while walking backwards in exasperation on a typical muggy summer day in Kyoto. I took the attitudes expressed in these and other conversations I overheard to heart and tried to understand what things people might really want to see and learn about. If that same young woman were to understand more precisely what life in a temple was like she might actually want to visit more of them.

I concluded generally that it was always useful to introduce people to uncommon places, or uncommon aspects of familiar ones often taken for granted and therefore easily neglected. Over the years, I occasionally joined tours in various parts of Kansai. From these experiences, I learned that official Japanese tour guides sometimes engaged in forms of cultural sanitation whereby certain behaviors might be glossed over by relegating them to the remote past. Especially if foreigners were present, the consequence might turn out to be a whitewashing of the present. On a visit to the Imperial Palace, for example, our guide told us that Shinto gates were painted vermilion because "in the olden times Japanese people *used to believe* in evil spirits" and the color kept the maleficent specters at bay. Yet at the end of the day, most of the Japanese I knew were afraid of jinxes and believed in spirits in one form or another. In their lives they took visible protective measures such as hanging up amulets at home or in the car, wearing Buddhist wrist-rosaries, and attending fire ceremonies to appease unidentified spirits or those of their known ancestors. For whose benefit was it then to present Japan in a secular light?

These essays fall into six broad categories—nature, industry, place, arts, youth culture, and religion. This division serves only as a convenient reference for the reader who might like to skip around the book rather than read from cover to cover. The chapters are meant to present a subject and introduce at the very least, one related place to explore. When I introduce shops, as in the case of the chapter on Issey Miyake, this is because aside from the fashion designer's Tokyo museum—21_21 Design Sight—free-standing boutiques or those inside department stores are the only public places where it is possible to view his fashion collections. Or in the chapter on toilets, I would not expect everyone to be inspired to go on a religious retreat where toilet cleaning is the central spiritual practice. But just knowing about a utopian community that promotes this method as a means to diminish the ego helps sensitize the reader to the ways in which new spiritualities draw on tradition and certainly makes the next visit to the bathroom a lot more fun. It should also engender a greater appreciation of the fact that Japan simply has the most advanced toilet technology on the planet.

The chapter on Japanese cuisine raises an old question of native versus newcomer, an issue as relevant to people as to plants. At what point is an exotic cultivar or imported vegetable finally considered *Japanese*? Does it take thirty, a hundred, or perhaps two hundred years? In an age of intensifying globalization the flows of influence hardly ever move in one direction anymore. This is patently clear in the discussion about the father of Japanese animation—Tezuka Osamu—and the multiple cultural streams from which he drew. Cosplay represents another case of cultural interpenetration—an American export from the world of sci-fi conventions ricochets back to the U.S. after blossoming into a full-fledged subculture in Japan. Once re-imported here, cosplayers make every effort to preserve the distinctly Japanese orientation of the practice. Origins get lost and are perhaps meaningless in these cases.

New trends are always emerging and older ones morphing into new forms or disappearing altogether. Youth culture in particular is a huge shape-shifting category. Although I wrote about Lolita fashion, anime, and manga there is another trend gaining steady momentum that I reluctantly skipped over. The *Yama Gaaru* or Mountain Girl movement that has swept across the country has a lively and active group of young women in Kyoto. Into a single genre they combine outdoor sports such as trekking, climbing, and camping with fashion and spirituality. Mountain Girls dedicate themselves to learning outdoor survival skills that involve chainsaws and woodworking in order to build shelters in teams. These young women dress attractively in rustic-chic fashion of the sort found in upscale sports-stores such as Mont Bell. For treks they may use Nordic walking sticks, colorful and well-designed backpacks, and wear nearly weightless and quilted, knee-length wrap-around mountain-skirts. Their destinations are usually not the classic historical sites but instead one of the many designated power spots in the country.

The term "power spot" was first coined in the 1990s by psychic spoon-bending Kiyota Masuaki to refer to places where the earth is believed to emit a great spiritual healing energy. As the trend picked up books began to appear on the subject. Teruo Wakatsuki Yuu came up with seventy-nine such spots after traveling from Hokkaido to Okinawa. Power spot tourism has gained momentum in Japan especially among young people. Several of my female students liked to report on them. Three notable power spots included in many lists are: Mt. Fuji in the Kanto, Yakushima, an island off the southern tip of Kyushu with giant cryptomeria trees (the inspiration for the forest setting in Miyazaki Hayao's film *Princess Mononoke)*, and Ise Jingu, in Kansai's Mie prefecture, the Shinto shrine complex dedicated to the ancestress of the Japanese people—the sun goddess Amaterasu Omikami—who inhabits a symbolic realm of light, purity, and fertility. One of the features of this recent spiritual trend is that the destinations are not exclusively Japan-centered; power spots have a truly global range. Some Japanese books on the subject may recommend: Mt. Saint Michel in France, Ayers Rock in Australia, the red-rock monoliths of Sedona (Arizona), and the Egyptian pyramids.

Although I have not engaged in power spot tourism per se, I have no doubt discovered powerful spots in Kansai. Mt. Kurama in Kyoto would certainly be one of them. Buried in a mountain valley surrounded by forests is a hot spring with an outdoor bath. In autumn, kites whirl overhead and in winter snow falls softly but the tub is always piping hot. The mountain is also the place where the founder of *reiki*—Usui Mikao (1865-1926)—came to meditate. A follower of Tendai and later of Shingon Buddhism, Usui received his gift of healing-hands in this mountain in 1914. Though he ultimately left Kansai for Kanto where he opened a clinic in Tokyo to teach his system of *reiki*, from there his students spread his technique throughout the world. Like so many of Japan's tangible and intangible gifts to the world, this one, too, originated in Kansai.

When you arrive in Kansai the mountains and oceans will certainly be there to meet you, and in all likelihood the temples too, but many of the places described in this book—restaurants, cafes, and shops—are highly vulnerable to the vicissitudes of time. There may be changes in location, development projects beyond a proprietor's control, economic vagaries, or other unforeseen events in the decades to come. In spite of changes that may arise, may you always find what you are looking for from this day forward.

Notes

1 Sometimes Fukui, Tokushima, and Tottori are included as a part of Kansai.

References

Foundation for Kansai Region Promotion. Kansai Window. www.kansai.gr.jp/en/index.html

Ishikawa Eisuke. Japan in the Edo Period: An Ecologically Conscious Society (Oedo ekoroji jijo). Kodansha Publishing Co., Tokyo, 2000. http://www.resilience.org/stories/2005-04-05/japans-sustainable-society-edo-period-1603-1867

Maxwell, Catherine. "Japan's Regional Diversity: Kansai vs. Kanto," Omusubi No. 3. Sidney, 2005

Russel, Oland. The House of Mitsui. Little Brown and Company, Boston, 1939.

Sofue Takao. Kenminsei no Ningengaku. Chikuma Shobo. Tokyo, 2012.

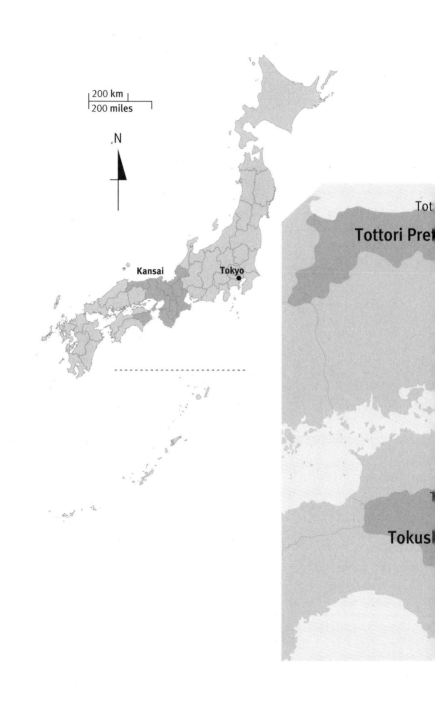

200 km
200 miles

N

Kansai   Tokyo

Tot
Tottori Pref

T
Tokus

PART I
NATURE

Gratitude
A Japanese Lesson

W HEN I FIRST CAME TO JAPAN, I was enchanted by the exquisite refinement of traditions such as the incense ceremony, and impressed by such singularities as the penchant to miniaturize—poems, trees, cars, and even whole landscapes. Like the sound of Basho's frog—stunning and evocative. Above all, the extraordinary appeal that Japan's religious traditions exerted on me remained a mystery to my Japanese friends and a veritable wedge between us. How could I explain my enthusiasm for the sheer abundance of forms of prayer, ritual, and meditation as found in the esoteric traditions of Shingon, Shugendo, and Tendai where mudras, mantras, and the 108-beaded *juzu* worked in tandem with cleansing waterfalls and purifying *goma* fires? All these seemed explicitly designed to engage the whole body with its myriad sensations and to quell busy minds and hearts through total engagement rather than austere renunciation. So swept up was I in new ways of thinking and feeling that I had room for little else. Only at unexpected moments—an incomprehensible phrase or a missed cue—would I realize with a shock that I was not Japanese after all and that

Izanagi and Izanami were not my mythical matrix. I can easily link this cognitive dissonance to the puzzle that ancestor veneration posed for me. It was a stumbling block that I could not seem to surmount because I lacked the experience that would allow me to grasp it.

During the year that I lived in the remote Goto Islands and did research on Japan's "Hidden Christians," I expected to find this community completely distinct from people of other religious traditions in these islands. The experience of persecution and secrecy had certainly isolated this group historically. But whether a Buddhist sect, a Shinto branch, a "Hidden Christian" village, a new, or a new-new religion, reverence for ancestors seemed perhaps the one common theme that could bind all these disparate strands and render them all transparently Japanese. Although ancestor veneration is a feature found in other civilizations as distinct as those of China and Africa, the puzzle that immediately confronted me was a Japanese one in all its concreteness. Closely related to ancestor reverence was the practice of "*kuyo*" or memorial services. I learned that just dying or being dead in itself, even for a very long time, would not automatically convert a person into an ancestor. According to some traditions, it took fifty years to become a true ancestor. During that time the potential ancestor was the object of great care, the recipient of numerous rites and offerings of fruit, incense, and scripture that would gradually refine the spirit and confer upon him or her the status of "ancestor." That was precisely the point—to be an ancestor was a status to achieve but it could not be done alone. It depended on the collaboration and goodwill of one's descendants. Various as they might be, these memorial practices constituted tangible links in a long chain that kept the past tightly fastened to the present.

The shift in my own consciousness towards an understanding of this cultural puzzle was a gradual one that laid the foundation for a radical change in my relationship with my own father. I attribute the possibility of such change ultimately to the persuasive influence of ancestor veneration on my own way of thinking.

As a point of reference, I can recall an incident that clearly exemplifies my original attitude. Returning to Hawai'i from Japan one Christmas, my younger brother, who was then studying to be a photographer, had discovered an old family photo. Enlarged to portrait-size, it became everyone's Christmas present that year. Taken at dockside at the close of the 19th century, this sepia photograph depicted our paternal ancestors. Headed for America from Ireland, they were dressed in old coats and odd caps, young and old, and surrounded by chunky leather suitcases. My first impression when I looked at this photo was: "Why on earth did my brother have to burden me with this?" The subtext to my annoyance was: "I have never met and never will meet these people, so I really have no relation to them." I told my mother she could keep my photo, too, because I had no place for it.

My little brother's gift had certainly not been prompted by any strain of ancestor reverence, but rather by a combination of retro-fashion and a post-Alex Haley search for "roots." In a country where nearly everyone originated from elsewhere, the demand to quickly shed one's past in order to become "American" resulted in a severing of the ancestors. In exchange, the "self-made" man or woman became a model of which "self-reliance" was the virtue.

One day my colleague at the pharmaceutical university in Tokyo where I was then employed asked me if I would be attending the "*dobutsu jikken kuyo*." I had never heard of such a *kuyo* before, but soon learned that twice a year the university conducted a memorial service for all the laboratory animals whose lives had been "sacrificed" for the benefit of science. That afternoon, under the shade of a huge tree on campus, all the laboratory employees turned up in their white lab coats. Although no "religious" official was present, a master of ceremonies made a short speech and then read from a white scroll that listed the kinds and precise numbers of animals that had been killed: guinea pigs 400, monkeys 22, mice 700, and so on. University staff members from other departments also attended the service and stood quietly with hands folded and heads bowed. The altar erected for the ceremony overflowed with offerings. A university administrator stood nearby with a bag of bananas and oranges and passed them out to participants who formed a long queue to the altar where each one placed fruit, and offered incense and a little prayer. The entire service took no more than forty-five minutes out of the usual working day.

Although the lives of various animals had been taken for laboratory experiments, the service implied that they had not been taken in vain. These lives were not simply used and forgotten, but remembered and honored with a precision that amounted to a ceremony of accountability. Although the expression of gratitude toward laboratory animals appeared wholly extraordinary to me at the time, I soon learned that this was just the tip of the iceberg in Japan. The more I looked around me, the more I discovered other equally remarkable examples of remembering and giving thanks. Japan's premiere pearl magnate—Mikimoto—conducts an annual memorial service for oysters. When asking about this practice, a company representative responded with the logic of a syllogism. The company makes its living from selling pearls and the pearls came from oysters. The *kuyo* follows naturally from those facts. I found myself agreeing wholeheartedly and felt embarrassed that I had ever posed such a question. Several years later, I was walking through Koyasan's illustrious cemetery—a who's who of Japanese historical personages. Among the tombs of emperors and shogun, I came across a remarkable sight—a large stone erected by a fumigation company, dedicated to white ants. The cultural refrain was becoming more audible now—lives taken to sustain other lives may be an inevitable human predicament, but they should nevertheless be fully acknowledged and honored.

I soon learned that memorials extended into the plant kingdom and far beyond. I witnessed a memorial service for chrysanthemums and heard of another for cherry trees whose wood had been used to make the lovely cylinder tea caddies found in many Japanese homes. More surprising yet was the fact that "inanimate objects" were likewise not exempt from ceremonious remembering. This completely smudged the line that I had always been taught divided the "animate" from the "inanimate" world. At a Buddhist temple, I watched the priests in their brocaded finery conduct a memorial service for sewing needles and chant sutras for their repose. Having saved broken needles throughout the year for this annual event, the participants, who were mostly seamstresses, now placed their broken or blunted needles into a soft bed of fresh tofu on the altar. This was so persuasive that I found myself thinking that if I were a broken needle, I would also like to rest in a soothing loaf of tofu. Thus, these rites serve to cultivate empathy in both the participants and observers. Whether a Buddhist *kuyo* for needles, a Shinto service for old combs, a *yamabushi* bonfire for stubby calligraphy brushes, or secular services offered by scientists for laboratory animals, nothing in Japan is deemed too small or trivial to be the object of a *kuyo*. More than any other single practice, this one highlights the profound sense of gratitude that permeates Japanese culture as a whole. Beneath this sentiment lies a worldview that considers all things interconnected.

By the time I next returned to Hawai'i for the Christmas holidays, I had observed numerous *kuyo* in Japan. But it was here at home where these experiences bore their first fruits. My father and I sat quietly across from each other in our living room one Sunday swapping portions of the newspaper. At a certain point, I looked up and noticed the striking resemblance of his foot to my own. For the first time in my life, it hit me like an electric shock that my father and I were actually made of the same flesh. To any observer, this would have been an obvious enough fact given that we were father and daughter. Yet I had never actually "experienced" this fact until that moment. Uttering to myself, "This is my father!" was nothing less than an epiphany and a definitive turning point in my life. While the English language falls short here, Japanese has the perfect words to express my feelings of gratitude upon realizing that the person in front of me was largely responsible for the very fact that I had a body at all. Those words are "*okagesama de.*" People use these words every day in Japan as a response to the familiar question: "*Ogenki desu ka*?" "*Hai, genki desu. Okagesama de.*" This phrase not only expresses the sense of interconnectedness of people, but reaffirms it countless times in the daily round of exchanges. Other linguistic compounds formed with "*itadaku,*" "*kureru,*" and "*kudasaru*" likewise reinforce the sense of being a grateful recipient. In my own case, that brief moment of reflexivity was the start of a translation into my own cultural idiom of the many *kuyo* I had witnessed. Ultimately, it served as a kind of initiation that allowed me to understand the meaning of ancestor veneration as the chain of such relationships as the one I had just experienced with my father, but reiterated over generations into the remote past. This awareness was only possible because of the initial conundrum that ancestor veneration had posed for me.

Not limited to *kuyo*, gratitude is a cultural theme that traverses every domain in Japanese society. The indigenous psychotherapy known as "Naikan" exploits this theme exclusively in the healing of various illnesses. Used in Japanese prisons and hospitals to reform or rehabilitate, Naikan is a method of rigorous self-reflection based on the philosophy that humans are fundamentally in debt since all existence implies mutual dependency. Even though humans are cared for in numerous visible and palpable ways by others from birth, they still tend to systematically forget the many acts of kindness they have received. Naikan addresses this issue through a structured meditation on just three questions: What did I receive? What did I give? What trouble did I cause? Beginning with the focus on one's mother, the Naikan client sits in front of a white "*byobu*" or screen from 6:30 a.m. until 9 p.m. for a period of one week engaged in a relentless recall of memories from birth to the present moment. The meditation is divided into three-year segments punctuated by five-minute visits every few hours from the Naikan therapist who asks just one question: "What did you examine?" Besides these brief interviews, Naikan tapes broadcast into one's room during mealtimes provide the only other external stimulus. These testimonials are passionate narratives of people who have discovered through Naikan the buried treasures in the invisible world of their own hearts and emerge from the Naikan "practice" with a cleansed attitude that drastically improves their psychological state and social relations. In the case of incurable diseases, at least the spirit of the person, if not the illness itself, can be healed through the cultivation of gratitude. If one can manage to survive the fatigue, boredom, and resistance that constitute the first three days of Naikan, then vivid memories begin to well up and flood the consciousness. By the time one has itemized the expenses parents have incurred from a diaper count through college tuition, the notion of a self-made man or woman seems a convenient but absurd fiction. For everything in one's existence is necessarily "*okage de*" to someone or some thing.

Visitors to Japan will justifiably continue to be dazzled as I was by the multiplicity of cultural forms. The juxtaposition of the ancient and the modern and the secular and the religious is so compelling that it is tempting to view Japanese culture in terms of rupture and discontinuity. At least that would be one way of explaining what appear to be simultaneous yet mutually exclusive worlds. However, underlying this apparent discontinuity lies a continuity of values that gives body to the many distinct forms whether they be old or new. Japan's cultural reservoir is deep and rich, and has proven its resilience and creativity historically through the ability to reinvent itself according to the demands and spirit of the times. This reinvention is never arbitrary but draws from a repertoire of values among which gratitude has long held a preeminent position in Japan. As gratitude affirms not only the complex web of human relations, but also those with the environment, it is as relevant to ancient Yamato as to postmodern Japan. My own debt to Japan for having taught me this precious lesson in gratitude is something that I will never be able to fully repay. But at least I can begin by acknowledging the debt.

Practical Information

Naikan Center
227 Gakuen Daiwa-cho, 3-chome
Nara-shi 631-0041
TEL 0742-48-2968
http://www4.ocn.ne.jp/~naikan/eng-06.html

The Ways of Water
Kyoto's Water Culture

KYOTO—ONE OF THE WORLD'S RICHEST CULTURAL CIT-
IES—is usually associated with famous temples and shrines,
not to mention great works of art, but it is above all a "water
city" for those who live here. The presence and abundance of
clear and flowing water, always within view, has profoundly influenced both the material and spiritual lives of the people. Though
physical environment certainly shapes human culture, it never
determines the outcome in any strict sense. Offering suggestions
and possible directions, human ingenuity takes over from there.
In the case of Kyoto, surrounded on three sides by hills that feed
water into the city, the dynamism and gracefulness that collectively characterize these many rivers, streams, brooks, and canals
that traverse the city at every turn have left heir imprint through
the creation of a strong yet fluid culture.

The cultural dimensions inspired by the nature of water
include the culinary, religious, aesthetic, industrial and moral. In
terms of food, tofu, rice, sake, tea and sweets are all intimately
related to the purity and abundance of the city's water. To the
touch, much of Kyoto's water feels almost silky, and to the taste

it can be earthy, woodsy, or have a kind of transparent flavor. The last type allows the water to bring out the natural flavors in other ingredients. Thus, the delicate Kyoto cuisine developed as a water-based diet with vegetables and tofu (composed largely of water), at its core. The traditional tea ceremony with its minimalist components is almost unthinkable without water of a quality able to stand on its own merit.

Exciting and excitable, water is always going somewhere. The perpetually changing surface of running waters gave to Buddhist ideas of impermanence a positive and creative charge (in contrast to the negative ephemera of falling cherry blossoms). Ponds and waterfalls became not only integral features of temple gardens, but were designed so that their wind-rippled surfaces would cast a fascinating play of shadows on paper windowpanes of nearby temples and villas as they do at Ginkakuji temple. The austerity of dry rock gardens conjures the presence of water abstractly through the skillful placement of sand and stones to suggest the waves and whirlpools of distance oceans. The Shinto, Buddhist, and Shugendo practice of *misogi* or spiritual cleansing through standing under a waterfall, or dousing oneself with buckets of bracingly cold water, derives from the deep desire to be united with the clarity and purity of water. Water by its very nature changes form according to the container in which it is placed. This quality suggested the Buddhist wisdom of the emptiness of form, and the social value of flexibility and a situational ethic over an unchanging stance for all occasions.

Aside from taste, sight, and touch, the sound of water is also important in Kyoto's water culture. Several inventions are used to capture its sound. The *sui-kin-kutsu* is a musical instrument played by water as it drips into an overturned perforated bottle buried underground such as found at Eikando temple. As droplets fall languorously through the hole, the bottle resonates like music from a dragon's chamber. The *sozu*, a miniature bamboo seesaw poised above a basin in a balancing act played by water alternately spilling from each end, is Kyoto's version of a scarecrow. Its loud rhythmical, and never-ending clacking characterizes the sound of summertime in the city.

Kyoto has flourished for 1,200 years nurtured by a series of underground streams that drain from the hillsides and bubble up from the subterranean depths of the earth. In fact, the city sits on top of a buried treasure—an enormous underground water reservoir 12 kilometers (about 7.5 miles) east-west and 33 kilometers (about 20.5 miles) north-south that holds 27.5 billion cubic meters of water. The mother lode of this vast water network forms an area in the heart of the city with Shimogamo Shrine, the Imperial Palace and Shinsen-en defining its boundaries.

Located at the confluence of Takano and Kamo rivers, Shimogawa Shrine has long served as the guardian of Kyoto's waters. In fact, the protection and management of water is usually associated with Shinto shrines where water is often plentiful, so that even today many residents (including myself) get their drinking water from wells at shrines famous for their water alone. The water at Nashi-no-ki Shrine, located near the Imperial Palace, is so popular that sometimes people need to wait in queue to draw the water. But countless lesser-known yet fully potable waters are cherished in their neighborhoods alone.

In the 19th century, when the capital of Japan moved from Kyoto to Tokyo, the ancient city responded to this desertion through the idiom of water. It reinvented itself as modern by forging a major new waterway—the Lake Biwa Canal that now links Kyoto to the largest lake in Japan and is the current source of the city's tap water. The city's next large-scale project—the construction of the underground subway system in the 1950s—severed some of these vital water veins that led to the drying up of some of the city's venerable water resources to the chagrin of local tofu makers who depended on it.

Kyoto's development continues to have a profound effect on the underground water system, the source of the city's cultural identity. The public protests in 2010-2011 to the building of a massive aquarium in Umekoji Park drove home just how sensitive the subject of tampering with the ancient water system can get. In some cases, water may be rejuvenated. Parts of the Horikawa river, buried for fifty-five years under tons of concrete, are now flowing again above ground along certain stretches. This river was and still remains the center of *yuzen* dyeing, a process now prohibited that once required placing long bolts of silk fabric on the surface of the flowing water to remove excess dye in order to achieve the vibrant colors for which it is known.

Kyoto actively struggles to reconcile its desire for development with the need for historical preservation, and water is crucial part of its cultural memory. Of all the pleasures of living in a city as ancient as Kyoto, the constant sight and sound of water is perhaps the greatest. From the larger river bodies of the Kamo, Takano, Katsura, or Shirakawa (including the more distant Hozu and Uji) to the major streams such as Takase, Misosogi and the various Biwa branch canals, water flows ceaselessly. Even cemeteries memorialize it in the tiered stone stupas that represent the five phases of the universe with various geometrical shapes. Coming after the cube for the earth is a sphere that stands for water. A single sparkling droplet subject to change, and essential for all life: This is water.

Practical Information

Nashi-no-ki Shrine
680 Somedonocho
Hirokoji-agaru, Teramachi-dori
Kamigyo-ku, Kyoto 602-0844
Tel: (075) 211-0885
www.nashinoki.jp

Eikando Temple
48 Eikando-cho
Sakyo-ku, Kyoto 606-8445
Tel: (075) 761-0007
www.eikando.or.jp

The Spirit of Bamboo

There is a saying: "In great storms trees break, but the supple bamboo bends." The strength that lies at the heart of such flexibility is what makes bamboo such a great material, and one that keeps turning up in unexpected guises—as a prime construction material in contemporary vernacular architecture or in soft bamboo rayon garments that easily drape.

A member of the grass family, bamboo is said to grow faster than any other plant in the world and, like a bird's bones, its hollow stalks make it very light. Ubiquitous in Japan, bamboo comes in an astounding array of colors: deep lacquer black, silvery-blue, jade-green, yellow, brown, and even striped.

It is used in weaving baskets as intricate as knitwear, and as sturdy ribbing for fans and umbrellas. Its upper brush makes excellent fences tied with hemp, and the plant's many root stubs are left on the flared end of the shakuhachi flute for their sheer finesse. Bamboo charcoal purifies water and deodorizes air, and takenoko bamboo shoots cooked as tempura have a flavor as delicate as artichoke hearts.

The one-room museum in Rakusai Bamboo Park in Nishikyo

Ward, Kyoto, even houses the crumbling remains of a bamboo plumbing system from the eighth century. But the story I found most compelling of all, and the one that subsequently led me on a quest, was the counterintuitive connection between the American inventor, Thomas Edison (1847-1931), and the bamboo of Kyoto.

According to a description at the museum, Edison was trying to find a filament that would burn long enough to be of practical value for his invention—the electric light bulb. From his New Jersey lab, the great inventor sent scouts to various countries in search of an appropriate material, and ultimately tested the fibers of about 6,000 plants.

The one that proved to burn the longest happened to grow in the bamboo groves of Yawata, Kyoto Prefecture. The *madake* bamboo (*Phyllostachys bambusoides*) burned a record 2,450 hours. That was the beginning of the global electrical revolution. The inventor then founded the Edison Electric Light Co. to manufacture the electric light bulbs with bamboo filaments from Kyoto. According to Thomas Edison, a biography by Charles E. Pederson, in 1883, Macy's department store in New York became the first business to use the incandescent light bulbs.

But a personal motive was actually driving my interest in the Edison story. My grandfather, who came to the United States through Ellis Island in 1900 with his parents and siblings from central Italy, worked as a draftsman for 47 years for General Electric Co., a company created through a merger in 1892, and helped redesign the GE logo. I knew vaguely that Edison had become the object of worship for a Japanese religious group called Denshinkyo or "electric gods," but had never met anyone remotely involved.

According to a newspaper article in 1949, a Japanese ministry granted the group official status after deliberating whether it was Buddhist, Shinto or something else. As the group's object of worship was "*Edison-no-mikoto*" ("*mikoto*" is a suffix used for deities) the ministry identified it as Shinto. The religion would give people the opportunity to express gratitude for the benefits of electricity, peace and scientific knowledge.

The walk from Yawata Station to Iwashimizu Hachimangu shrine, down Edison Road and past a bust of Thomas Edison, took about 20 minutes. Established in 859, the shrine is located on top of Otokoyama, a mountain lush with bamboo groves in which Edison's scout found the bamboo for the filament that would open the age of electricity. The shrine is considered the southern gate that warded off evil from the ancient capital of Kyoto, while the northern gate is Enrakuji temple on Mt. Hiei. Not only is there a monument dedicated to Edison on the shrine grounds, but since 1934, two festivals a year are held in his honor.

Edison's birthday on February 11 happens to fall on National Founding Day when Shinto shrines celebrate the "birth" of the country and offer prayers for the prosperity of the nation. At Iwashimizu Hachimangu, the celebration is followed at noon by a gathering of shrine priests, staff and local people to give thanks to Thomas Edison. I joined them this year with the thought of how much the whole story would have pleased my grandfather.

However, this shrine did not have any connection with Denshinkyo, and the priest there did not know anyone from the now

defunct religious group. What is more confusing is that there were several secular groups devoted to Edison, such as the Kyoto Yawata Edison Association and the Edison Admiration Society.

"Is Edison a god?" I asked Norito Sakurai, a young priest.

"In the past, Edison might have been deified, but not now," Sakurai said as he stopped to reflect for a moment. "The base of Shinto is that we humans manage to live because of water, trees, and nature. We're expressing a deep gratitude that goes beyond the nation. Through Edison's invention and genius, people's lives were enriched. He gave us light. And that was initially made possible from the nature around this shrine."

Here nature and a flexible human intelligence are seen to work together. His almost superhuman grasp of nature's secrets makes Edison irresistible in Japan. I soon discovered that Iwashimizu Hachimangu was not the only shrine to be associated with Edison. In nearby Arashiyama, on the precincts of the Shingon temple Horinji, is a Shinto shrine called Dendengu devoted to Denden Myojin, the ancestral god of electronics. Here, Edison together with the German scientist Heinrich Rudolf Hertz (1857-1894), who discovered electromagnetic waves, are both memorialized with a stone pagoda and monument.

On my way home from visiting the shrine, I stopped at Kagoshin on the north side of Sanjo Street a 10-minute walk east of the Kamogawa river. The shop has been in operation since 1862 when the whole area buzzed and snapped with the sound of bamboo craftwork. Now only two shops, surrounded by modern buildings, remain on what was once part of the Tokaido highway. Shintaro Morita, a fifth-generation master bamboo artisan, is turning out baskets and vases. His daughter Tsuyako works beside him, runs the shop, and deals with the public.

"In autumn, we cut the bamboo," she says, "and in February and March we make things." Most of what they use is *madake*, the same bamboo used by Edison.

"Edison sent people to our shop to ask about bamboo, too," Tsuyako says beaming. Since GE continued to send Christmas cards to the family over the years, I told her about my grandfather and his hand in the GE logo.

Our exchange allowed me to better understand the thinking in a place like Kyoto. Relations between people, and perhaps it holds for nations as well, are like the rhizomes of bamboo that travel underground, sometimes over great distances.

Practical Information

Rakusai Bamboo Park

300-1 Kitafukunishi-cho, Ohe
Nishikyo-ku, Kyoto 610-1112
Tel: (075) 331-3821
www.17.ocn.ne.jp/~park/English.html

Kinsuitei Restaurant (specializes in takenoko cuisine)

2-15-15 Tenjin, Nagaokakyo-shi
Kyoto 617-0824.
Tel: (075) 951-5151
www.kinsuitei.co.jp

Iwashimizu Hachimangu shrine

(Feb. 11: Edison's birthday; Oct 18: Edison's memorial service)
30 Yawata, Kobo, Yawata-shi
Kyoto 614-8005.
Tel: (075) 981-3001
www.iwashimizu.or.jp.

Horinji temple

68-3 Arashiyam Kokuzoyamacho
Nishikyo-ku, Kyoto 616-0006
Tel: (075) 861-0069

Kitahara Seikado (Shakuhachi maker)
36 Kagamiyacho-agaru, Ebisugawa
Muromachi-dori, Nakagyo-ku, Kyoto 604-0002
Tel: (075) 231-2670
www.k-seikado.com

Kagoshin (bambooware)
Higashiyama Ward, Kyoto
9 a.m. to 6 p.m. daily
Tel: (075) 771-0209

Listening to Incense

T HE WORLD OF INCENSE is full of evocative power that can conjure up striking primordial imagery. The golden resin known as frankincense comes from a tree that grows in some of the most forbidding landscapes, and ambergris from the remains of squid beaks excreted by sperm whales. And *jinko* or aloeswood is the immune response of a tropical Southeast Asian tree to a life-threatening fungal infection.

Jinko, together with sandalwood, comprise the aromatic core of traditional Japanese incense in the form of sticks, pellets, coils or powder. *Nihon Shoki* (Chronicles of Japan) offers the country's first report of the fragrant wood, said to have drifted ashore on Awajishima island in Hyogo Prefecture in 595. The residents of the island between Honshu and Shikoku are said to have begun burning their find as firewood, but astonished by the fragrance, put out the fire, and instead presented the wood to the Imperial Court in Nara. Prince Shotoku recognized the resinous wood as precious aloeswood whose resinous core is "*kyara*," the crème de la crème of incense wood.

To this day on the northwestern shore of Awajishima, the

Kareki Shrine facing the Seto Inland Sea enshrines *jinko* as its object of veneration. The island is also home to incense maker Kunjudo, established in the Meiji era (1868-1912), which offers workshops in making cone and pressed incense. According to Shozo Akashi of Kunjudo, the island produces about 70 percent of Japan's incense. The hub of this production is the town of Ei, where over half the population is involved in the industry. The flourishing industry is partly attributable to the scant rainfall and seasonal west wind on the island that provide ideal conditions for drying incense.

Incense and Buddhism

The culture of incense in Japan developed in tandem with Buddhism and traditional Chinese medicine. Incense was required for religious rituals where it purified the air and marked the passing of the hours with sticks or incense trails made to measure. It also did duty as an insect repellent for the preservation of sutra texts and Buddhist vestments. Clove, sandalwood, and camphor are especially effective and constitute major ingredients in the sachets produced by all of Japan's major incense companies even today.

As healing inevitably involves both body and spirit, blurry lines existed from the start within the triad of Buddhism, medicine and incense. Kungyokudo Co., a Kyoto incense seller opposite Nishi Hongwanji temple, which it supplies, was first established as a pharmacy of Chinese medicine in 1594. The company's director, Hiroki Yamaguchi, said: "At first the incense ingredients were considered medicinal. *Jinko* was thought to be good for blood pressure and was consumed rather than enjoyed as a fragrance."

It is hardly by chance that Shoyeido Incense Co., a distinguished incense dynasty since 1705 and creator of such hits as Horikawa, is located on Nijo street. This is an area of Kyoto where clove merchants who imported Chinese medicines through the ports of Nagasaki and Okinawa prefectures once thrived. As incense makers, the Hata family could more easily procure the ingredients for blends that a third-generation family member had learned while working in the nearby Imperial Palace.

The Chinese monk Ganjin (688-763), also known as Jianzhen, who is usually credited with the introduction of incense to Japan, arrived in the archipelago in 754 during the early wave of Nara Buddhism. He propagated the Ritsu school of Buddhism and introduced incense recipes and materials, influencing the spherical shape in which incense would be made, its rich blends and the traditional method of indirect burning by burying a tiny charcoal briquette in a cup of ash.

As in China, the use of incense in Japan spilled over from the religious sphere into the secular. Aromatic materials that release fragrant smoke when burned involve the skill of artisans coupled with spiritual and artistic imagination. Thus, kodo or "the way of fragrance" began in the Heian period (794-1192) but became a formal art in the Muromachi period (1336-1573) as a ceremonial way of "listening to incense." The ritual required minute preparations of the incense cup with special tools to form an ash mountain with a tiny mica slab on the peak, on which a miniscule square wood chip or incense pellet would be placed for indirect burning. This developed into various incense pass times in which participants competed to produce the best fragrance or played guess-the-scent games.

The eighth shogun of the Muromachi shogunate, Ashikaga Yoshimasa (1436-1490), was a devotee of the incense ceremony and collected fragrant woods. In his villa in the Higashiyama hills in Kyoto, now known as Ginkakuji temple, or the Silver pavilion, the retired shogun had an incense ceremony room—the Roseitei—the only one that still exists from antiquity today.

Yet the refined art of incense, like most of Japanese culture, remained hidden from the world and was long exoticized. It took the Chicago World's Fair in 1893 to open the floodgates. Along with Zen, Japanese incense also made its debut on the world stage at this time.

Hands-on Incense Blending

The continuing passion for incense in Japan is intimately connected to the spiritual sustenance that the mixing of several ingredients from nature's treasure chest—or the showcasing of a single one—has provided for centuries. This became crystal clear to me during an incense-making workshop given by Yamada-Matsu Co. in Kyoto, a seller of natural extracts, medicine and fragrant woods located west of the Kyoto Imperial Palace. The store has hundreds of drawers along one wall, an enormous helical narwhal tusk on another and boxes of Buddhist rosaries made of various fragrant woods.

Nine of us were led to a back room to make traditional black, pellet-shaped incense soft as clay according to a recipe that included nine ingredients plus three of our own choosing, with musk being an option. With a base of *jinko* and sandalwood, we added clove, Borneo camphor, spikenard, pistachio, *sumi* to impart a uniform blackness, plum water to blend, and ground cuddy shell to bind them all together. The mood was intense, the excitement palpable, and no two people came up with the same incense blend.

Japan's major incense producers are highly innovative. Along with their own traditional blends for Buddhist altars and ceremonies, they experiment with modern lines that include producing scents as novel as coffee, green tea, grapefruit and even double mint. Do not, however, jump to easy conclusions. Coffee incense is not made from any part of the coffee plan but rather is conceptual and creates the mood rather than the aroma of coffee. Incense makers are designers no less than those in the fashion world, though they deal in the most ethereal and ephemeral of fabrics. Marilyn Monroe said it all when she famously remarked that all she wore to bed was Chanel No. 5. No comment makes a bolder suggestion that fragrance is not an accessory but something as fundamental and primary as a garment.

Practical Information

Kunjudo
1255-1 Taga, Awaji-shi, Hyogo 656-1521
Tel: (0799) 85-1301
www.kunjudo.co.jp

Kungyokudo Co.
Nishi Hongwanji-mae, Horikawa-dori
Shimogyo-ku, Kyoto 600-8349
Tel: (075) 371-0162
www.kungyokudo.co.jp

Shoyeido Incense Co.
Nijo-agaru, Karasuma-dori
Nakagyo-ku, Kyoto 604-0857
Tel: (075) 212-5590
www.shoyeido.com

Ginkakuji temple (Silver Pavilion)
Roseitei Incense Room
1 Ginkakujicho, Sakyo-ku, Kyoto 606-8402
Tel: (075) 771-5725

Yamada-Matsu Co.
164 Kageyukoji-cho
Kamigyo-ku, Kyoto 602-8014
Tel: 075) 441-4694
www.yamadamatsu.co.jp

Baieido Co.
1-4-1 Kurumano-cho Higashi
Sakai-shi, Osaka 590-0943
Tel: (722) 29-4545
www.baieido.co.jp

Mother of Pearls
Lake Biwa

L AKE BIWA IS SYNONYMOUS WITH PEARLS. Japan's largest body of freshwater, between 4 million and 5 million years old, the lake lies in the center of Shiga Prefecture, near Kyoto City. It was here that freshwater pearl cultivation first began. Beginning in the 1890s, a flurry of Japanese researchers began to experiment with pearl cultivation, first with oysters in Mie Prefecture's Ago Bay and later with mussels in Lake Biwa.

Not until 1910 did the first cultured freshwater pearls of any commercial value begin to appear. Though not the originator of the technique, it is largely because of the commercial genius of Kokichi Mikimoto (1858-1954) that it is possible to speak of a "cultural revolution" in the jewelry industry that drove pearl ownership out of the domain of the rich few and made the single classic strand of pearls affordable for the full-time homemaker and working woman alike.

According to sources including the Mikimoto Pearl Island Co., Mikimoto and his associates produced pearls by inserting a piece of tissue (not a bead as in oyster pearls) into the fleshy mantle of a mussel. As would happen with a naturally occurring sand grain, this irritant acts as a catalyst to stimulate the mussel to produce a pearly substance known as nacre or mother of pearl. Mussel shells themselves are made of nacre, visible in the inner iridescent lining of each half-shell. In the case of a pearl, the progressive accumulation of many concentric layers of nacre around the invasive particle creates the distinctive iridescence or rainbow effect known as "orient," which is one of the measures of a pearl's value.

Biwa pearls appeared on the scene just when the natural saltwater pearl industry was in serious global decline. Mikimoto's new technology dispensed with the need for pearl divers and added an extra advantage in the case of freshwater pearls: A single mussel could be seeded with multiple bits of tissue to produce as many as 20 pearls. From the consumer's perspective, at least part of the charm of these small freshwater gems called "Biwa pearls" was attributable to their unprecedented colors—mauve, peach, or heather, and their irregularities, though all were variations on a basic rice-grain shape. Designer Paloma Picasso—daughter of Pablo Picasso—was a devotee of Biwa pearls, and helped spread their popularity through her signature pieces of multiple strands twisted into single chunky necklaces known as torsades.

Even so, Mikimoto initially faced criticism on a global scale. Jewelers and consumers accused his cultured pearls of being "fake" because they were the product of human intervention rather than occurring naturally. But the genuine beauty and affordability of Mikimoto's pearls ultimately conquered the lingering resistance and for most of the 20th century Japan dominated the pearl industry. Given lake Biwa's fame as the mother lake of these pearls, people still often refer to any freshwater pearl simply as a "Biwa" no matter what its place of origin.

The area of Omihachiman on the eastern shore of Lake Biwa had most of the pearl farms, though today their production is negligible. Most of the *naiko* or inner harbors where many pearl farms once operated were filled in to produce land for more rice paddies in a trend that started in the 1970s, according to Michio Kumagai, senior research scientist at the Lake Biwa Environmental Research Institute. Aside from reclaimed land, by the late 1970s the many holiday resorts, agricultural chemicals, and industries surrounding the water began to take their toll on the lake, and the center of gravity of the pearl industry shifted to China.

But pearls or no pearls, homage to Lake Biwa is probably as old as the human communities that settled along the lakeshore about 20,000 years ago. According to the origin myth of the lake, Mt. Fuji and Lake Biwa share a deep connection. After a thunderous earthquake and torrential rains, the skies were said to have cleared and revealed an immense sheet of blue covering the land while simultaneously on the distant Suruga plain the mountain we know as Mt. Fuji exploded into existence. From a hilltop in the Omi domain (present-day Shiga Prefecture) amazed observers noticed that the shape of the lake resembled the Chinese four-stringed lute called a "*biwa*" in Japanese, from which the serene body of water derives its name.

Lake Biwa is home to four islands—Chikubushima, Okishima, Takeshima and Okinoshiraishi. Only the second has a sizable community, while the first, located in the central northern part of the lake, is a major pilgrimage destination. Chikubushima's eighth-century Buddhist temple of Hogonji enshrines both Kannon and Benzaiten. The latter is a deity of eloquence and music (usually depicted with a lute in hand), and her original Sanskrit name means "one having water." Indeed, today Lake Biwa provides water for 14 million people in the region.

The lake and the region of the Omi domain were immortalized in poetry long before pearls entered their history. By the 17th century, the *Omi Hakkei* (Eight Views of Omi) had become a literary and artistic convention. The *ukiyo-e* master Utagawa (or Ando) Hiroshige (1797-1858), for example, produced his own *Omi Hakkei*, a series of landscapes focused on scenic spots along the southern shoreline.

The subject of art and poetry, and the foundation of human sustenance for millennia, Lake Biwa, fed by hundreds of brooks and rivers and home to over a thousand species of plants and animals, is truly Japan's mother lake. In every season but winter it is possible to ride a bicycle around the entire girth in a few days. But in winter, when the snows deepen and the northern passage is forbidding, Lake Biwa can just be admired. It often glows then with the iridescent serenity of a giant blue pearl.

Practical Information

Lake Biwa Museum
1091 Oroshimo, Kusatsu
Shiga 525-0001
Tel: (077) 568-4811
www.lbm.go.jp/english

Sagawa Art Museum
2891 Kitagawa, Mizuho-cho
Moriyama-shi, Shiga 524-0102
Tel: (077) 585-7800.
www.sagawa-artmuseum.or.jp/

Biwako Visitors Bureau
Collabo Shiga 21, 6th Fl
2-1 Uchidehama, Otsu
Shiga 520-0806
Tel: (077) 511-1530
www.biwako-visitors.jp/

PART II
INDUSTRY

The Obi of Kyoto
Tied to Tradition
Future Bound

W ERE THE FASHION INDUSTRY to keep a list of endangered species of clothing, the *obi* would appear there along with the Austrian dirndl and the Scottish kilt. Yet it is unthinkable that the long sash worn over the kimono would disappear altogether. As an essential item of the kimono ensemble, the *obi's* niche is secure at least as a ritual garment worn for weddings, flower arrangement exhibitions, tea or incense ceremonies, Noh and Kabuki performances—in short, any activity that requires the performance of *Japaneseness*.

Where the *obi* in partnership with the kimono has lost its ground is in the domain of daily wear. While the switch to modern Western dress began for Japanese men much earlier—in the Meiji era—Japanese women did not give up the *obi*-cinched kimono until the post war period. The reason for this gender discrepancy is partially explainable in aesthetic terms—women had much more to lose than men by giving up the traditional dress. Men's *obi* had hardly evolved since the end of the 15th century when the kimono's prototype—the *kosode* became the standard dress for both men and women. Men's *obi*, lacking in diversity and ornament, remained rudimentary. Fashioned from white, grey or black-hued silk, never more than 9 centimeters (about 3.5 inches) wide, men tied this sash in a simple half bow at the back or tucked it in at the waist.

In contrast, the female-oriented *obi* industry promoted the sash to cult status among Japanese women. Fasteners of coral or porcelain came to embellish the outer cord that held the *obi* in place. Tiny cushions filled out bows, and elaborate motifs of birds, flowers or trees stood out against a brilliant background of metallic thread. The manufacturers, designers, dyers and weavers responsible for *obi* production steadily refined the techniques originally imported from Korea and China in the eighth century. For hundreds of years the *obi* was fussed over so that both its size and position vacillated—tied in front, on the side or in the back. During the 18th century, there were more than 20 ways to tie the *obi* so that it could convey age, status, and availability much in the same way Spaniards once used the silent language of the fan.

By the mid-Edo (1603-1867), the *obi's* length and width had finally become standardized, as did its position. The rear style had proven itself the most stable, perhaps because of the increasing weight and bulk typical of the most ornate silk brocades. The *obi* had definitely become the centerpiece of the outfit, not only in the physical sense as the point that drew the eye's attention and divided the woman's body into two nearly equal parts, but because a single kimono could be worn with several different *obi* to convey various seasons or social messages. In this way, a collection of *obi* could vastly extend a limited kimono wardrobe.

Today, three main types of *obi* can be found in specialty shops, department stores, and flea markets in Kyoto. All three styles were popular in the "roaring twenties" of the Taisho era (1912-1926) and some of the most captivating kimono and *obi* combinations anywhere can be seen in Seijun Suzuki's surrealistic film series, "The Taisho Trilogy." As *obi* go, the most formal—the *maru obi*—made of the finest silk brocade, has a single seam sewn along its length that gives it a double thickness, and measures

420 centimeters (about 13.8 feet) in length and up to 68 centimeters (about 2.25 feet) in width when folded. However, its uncomfortable weight, stiffness and astronomical cost are the main reasons for its present scarcity. *The fukuro obi* shares the same dimensions as the *maru obi* but is lined with a mildly contrastive material. In this way, it is often reversible with plain silk or satin on the opposite side. Shorter than the other two, the Nagoya *obi* is folded over and stitched to make it easy to wear. Its convenience and brighter color palette appeal to young women and it is among the most popular *obi* on the market today.

For five centuries the neighborhood of Nishijin, west of the Imperial Palace in Kyoto, has been the production center of Japan's *obi*, silk brocades, twills and gauzes. Its narrow streets are lined with two-story wooden townhouses called *machiya*, the traditional habitations of the textile artisans and the merchants who organize production and sell the finished products to wholesalers. The characteristic latticed doors and house-fronts are often painted with a red-ocher pigment that repels moths from these silk-weaving workshops. "Nishijin" refers not only to this district in Kyoto, but to a weaving process and to a textile product that carries its label.

In pre-modern Japan, weaving was traditionally a man's occupation although women often prepared the looms and sat above them in order to batch the pre-dyed yarns in accordance with the design. Finally, in the 19th century, when Japan energetically embarked on its course of modernization, the government sent three textile experts from Kyoto to Lyon, France, to acquire new weaving technology. They returned with the jacquard mechanism, a system that used hundreds of punched cards to code designs and batch the threads of the handlooms. This mechanism and the subsequent introduction of power looms freed women from their previous role as human jacquards and allowed them to become *de facto* weavers. Later innovation would replace the old punch-card system with a computerized jacquard using floppy disks.

These technological innovations radically transformed the weaving industry of Nishijin from single-weaver households to a household production system in which whole families worked at home on looms either owned by the weaver or rented from the manufacturer. In both cases, although the weavers worked at home, manufacturers provided them with the raw materials and paid them by the piece. Small factories or workshops away from the home eventually developed in Nishijin in the postwar years with 10 to 20 weavers employed from nine to five and paid at an hourly rate.

In spite of the increasing workforce, the industry fell into decline in the 1980s with dozens of manufacturers forced to close each year and those lucky enough to survive pressed into a drastically curtailed production mode. The main reason for the decline was the accelerating shift in fashion from the ethnically defined kimono to ready-to-wear clothing and the dawning awareness of global designer labels. Manufacturers initially responded to the disappearing market by outsourcing. First they hired weavers in the Tango Peninsula, about 100 kilometers (about 62 miles) from Kyoto. Once known for its silk crepe, that industry had become depressed and weavers were eager for new work. Manufacturers went further still and contracted weavers in China, Korea and Taiwan.

Now, just when it seemed the *obi* had gone to join the *miyako* kingfisher (no longer seen in Japan's skies), recycled *obi* have started to turn up in various guises in the West. Sometimes they have been transformed beyond recognition and called into new service as decorative accents in homes. They lie stretched across slabs of mahogany as table runners. They are re-sewn into bedspreads, or refashioned into men's evening vests for a night at the opera. They adorn couches as cushion covers, and women are enjoying them as summer corset-tops. For dramatic effect, they are draped over bamboo rods and used as window treatments. They hang vertically from doors, are suspended from walls and wind around banisters of once-barren staircases. The

fukuro obi twisted in a loose spiral and placed in a glass tube becomes a stunning table centerpiece. In Honolulu, Anne Namba Designs specializes in "kimono couture," or garments made from vintage kimono and *obi*. The designer's clients have included Mikhail Baryshnikov and the late Elizabeth Taylor.

What some see as an honorable rescue mission that involves deconstruction and innovation others view less benignly. Organizations such as the Kyoto Kofu Hozonkai (Society for the Preservation of Traditional Dress), founded with the aim to both preserve the kimono and *obi* as they are and to promote them as daily wear, opposes such "reformations" as thoughtless destruction of cultural property. Between these two poles of innovation and preservation, still others have found a middle way. Tatsumua Textile Co in Nishijin, one of Kyoto's most distinguished weaving manufacturers, has long derived many of its designs from ancient patterns found in works of Nara's Shosoin and Horyuji temples. They employ handloom weavers who make traditional textiles but they also have not shied away from diversifying. Besides neckties, upholstery and tapestries for Gion Festival floats, they have provided textiles for seats on airlines ANA and JAL, and for Shinkansen trains.

Survival always demands adaptation. Perhaps the *obi* renaissance abroad will stimulate a reappraisal at home and the *obi* will be rediscovered in Japan. Once again it may adorn the body or at least the home.

Practical Information

Nishijin Textile Center
Horikawa-Imadegawa Minami-iru
Kamigyo-ku, Kyoto 602-8216
Tel. (075) 432-6131
www.nishijin.or.jp
(Master weavers at work, kimono fashion show, assortment of woven goods)

Kitano Tenmangu Shrine
931 Bakuro-cho
Kamigyo-ku, Kyoto 602-8386
Tel: (075) 461-0005
www.kitanotenmangu.or.jp
Tenjinsan Flea Market—monthly on the 25th
(Wide selection of second-hand obi)

Kyoto Society for the Preservation of Traditional Dress
(Kyoto Kofu-Hozonkai)
60 Kami-Minamida-cho,
Sakyo-ku, Kyoto 606-8405
Tel: (075) 761-3803
www.hozonkai.org
(Recycles vintage kimono and obi)

Pedaling Through Time
When The Bicycle Reached Japan

T HE IDEA OF A MECHANICAL HORSE, a beast that would require no oats, hoof-trimming or tooth-filing, was perhaps a collective dream during the transportation-frenzied 19th century that ushered in an age of global tourism. In Europe, the dream eventually gave birth to the modern bicycle, for which no single individual or nation can claim exclusive credit. What unfolded was a series of incremental improvements on an international scale. Japan became part of this process shortly after the bicycle entered the country in the 1860s.

The Shimano Foundation's Bicycle Museum Cycle Center in Sakai, Osaka Prefecture, owns a spiffy exemplar of the bicycle's early ancestor—the *draisienne*—an 1818 German invention with a long wooden body fitted with iron-belted wheels, a front steering device and no pedals at all. The rider would straddle a narrow leather saddle and move the vehicle forward by pushing along the ground with both feet. Though it was equipped with a rudimentary brake, conflicts with pedestrians were hardly uncommon. What's more, riders also easily wore out their boots. Thus, the draisienne enjoyed intense but brief popularity.

The French, English and Scottish made their own versions based on this prototype, embarking on three decades of kaleidoscopic experimentation. By 1839 something called a velocipede had emerged from the creative chaos. It had pedals and rotary cranks attached to a front wheel hub but the rider's feet were now fully off the ground, requiring a new sense of balance to negotiate the cobbled streets characteristic of many European cities. Since riding such a heavy two-wheeler was often a highly rattling experience, people called it "the boneshaker."

In Europe, the velocipede generated wild excitement with rinks and riding schools in many cities that mainly attracted adventurous young men. Blacksmiths also took up the challenge and jerry-rigged their own vehicles. Indeed, bicycles—with their frames made of sturdy metal tubes—opened up a whole new line of employment for gun makers in Britain, France and the United States, as would happen later in Japan.

But the basic problem with the velocipede was that it simply could not go fast enough. The invention of the high-wheeler or "ordinary"—a bicycle with an enormous front wheel and a small rear one—was meant to remedy this situation. These metal-framed bicycles with solid rubber tires became the racing bicycles of their day. The very large front wheel allowed greater distance to be traveled with each rotation. The downside was that the rider sat precariously perched at such a height above the ground that mounting and dismounting posed a serious hazard.

Sudden braking could easily flip the vehicle over or simply throw the rider. Disasters never seemed far away, as glimpsed in the classic 1956 film *Around the World in 80 Days* when the charming valet Passeportout careens through the streets of London on an ordinary and is ordered by a horse-and-buggy driver to move his "confounded contraption" before the two vehicles collide.

When bicycles first entered Japan in the 1860s with their Western owners, tricycles were particularly popular in Yokohama. According to Takeuchi Tsuneyoshi, a specialist in the bicycle's industrial history, bicycles evidently existed in sufficient numbers to warrant the Osaka prefectural police to enact traffic regulations in 1870 that included these new vehicles. Five years later, a tax of ¥1 was levied on all bicycle owners.

As in Europe and the United States, the bicycle industry in Japan benefitted from the presence of trained gunsmiths. Miyata Gun Manufacturing produced Japan's first modern or safety bicycles using the same gun-barrel piping for the frame. Even earlier, smaller enterprises had begun to make their own high-wheelers out of metal parts. In Japan, these bicycles with their striking silhouette were called *daruma-gata* after the great Buddhist practitioner Bodhidharma in his popular manifestation as a roly-poly Daruma good-luck doll with a large bulbous bottom and smaller head.

By far the most sensational *daruma-gata* of the day was a 1.3-meter (about 4.25 feet) Columbia high-wheeler the American Thomas Stevens rode through Japan in 1886 on an amazing 21,600-kilometer (about 13422 miles) ride around the world. Stevens cycled 1,280 kilometers (about 795 miles) across Japan, some of them along the ancient Tokaido road, at a time when bicycles were a high-tech status symbol.

Stevens was not only the first person to circle the globe by bicycle, but he accomplished this extraordinary feat on the most challenging vehicle of the time. Given the high-wheeler's limitations and rough terrain, he had to walk for about a third of his journey, as recounted in his memoir *From Teheran to Yokohama*, the second volume of *Around the World on a Bicycle* (1887).

From his arrival in Nagasaki by boat to his departure from Yokohama, the young American was the delight of Japanese paparazzi. The press was not alone in its fascination with the young American. According to Yukio Otsu, a researcher on the history of the Japanese ordinary, the last shogun—Tokugawa Yoshinobu—either witnessed Stevens along his route or read about him in newspaper coverage. In a report published in the *Shizuoka Daimu Shimbun* of February 1887, the shogun, famous for his admiration of modern gadgets, ordered a similar nickel-plated high-wheeler or himself immediately afterwards. The following year, Yoshinobu could be seen daily tooling about Shizuoka on his *daruma-gata* with a servant in tow.

A decade later, the bicycle scene in Japan had changed dramatically. The modern or safety bicycle, characterized by wheels of equal size, was being manufactured domestically. The central telegraph office in Tokyo and newspapers offices in Osaka both used bicycles for delivery. These "mechanical horses" were so popular that they began to edge out both rickshaws and buggies. When Sir John Fraser of England arrived in Japan with two other wheelmen on a world tour in 1896 on Rover safety bicycles, they found streets filled with a mixture of old, new and ad hoc. From Fraser's memoir—*Round the World on a Wheel* (1907)—it would seem that Nagoya ranked as the bicycle capital of the nation:

"I would like to have stayed a week in Nagoya enlightening my mind as to what a bicycle can be made of...The big wheel was usually a cast-off cart wheel, bound with iron, and maybe a couple of heavy wooden spokes missing. As a rule, the backbone was the branch of a tree...and the back wheels had, without exception, devoted their energies in prehistoric times to trundling a wheelbarrow. The seat consisted of a sack tied to the backbone...The rider, his kimono tied about his waist, would mount, wearing his big wooden clogs all the time, and gripping the handlebars and leaning well back was able to push splendidly...And the noise they made!.. And there were dozens, hundreds, thousands of these careering about Nagoya."

Since that time bicycles have undergone relentless transformations. Tsuneyoshi Takeuchi has noted that the earliest models were imports and intended less for private ownership than for hire. In the early 20th century, the Nagoyan bicycle entrepreneur Okamoto Matsuzo traveled to Britain, France, and Germany and purchased the latest production machinery for bicycles. Thus, during World War I, when bicycle imports were almost unobtainable, Japan possessed the technology that allowed the expansion of bicycle production. By the 1930s, bicycles were finally massproduced in Nagoya. This brought down their price to levels at which stores and restaurants began to depend on them for delivery. These early bicycles had no gears, possessed heavy frames, and had large rear carriers to bear the weight of their loads.

At the cycle History Conference held in Osaka in 2000, Ross D. Petty reported that at the outbreak of World War II there were about 10 million bicycles in Japan. Half of these disappeared during the war and many that survived had to make do with ropes and hoses for tires.

After the postwar reconstruction period, the concept of bicycle shifted from the pragmatic to a hybrid of recreational and practical. Affordable easy-to-ride mini-cycles with 50-centimeter wheels drew many women into the bicycle fold. The *mama-chari* or "mama-chariot," a bicycle with a basket in front and a baby seat behind became widespread and remains so today. Shimano Inc. is a world leader in high-quality bicycle parts, having designed the first sturdy gear system for mountain bicycles to withstand mud, water and grit.

The dream of the "mechanical horse" reared its head in 2011 with an interesting new twist. The March 11 earthquake and tsunami that devastated northern Japan also brought the subway and train system of the nation's capital to a halt. About 8 million commuters were temporarily stranded with few and unappealing options—a long walk home, several hours wait for a cab or a night in a hotel. These extraordinary circumstances evidently led to a lifestyle reassessment reflected in a subsequent spike in bicycle purchases. According to a Bloomberg news report, the Osaka-based Asahi Co., doubled its bicycle sales in the month following the quake, and revenues for the Japan unit of Taiwan's Giant Manufacturing Co., the world's largest bicycle maker, rose 23 percent in March of that year.

In some Japanese cities such as Kyoto, the bicycle serves as a major means of transportation, and adequate infrastructure supports this choice. Bicycle paths along the city's many waterways minimize conflict with traffic and add an edge of intimacy to urban life. Organizations such as the Kyoto Cycling Tour Project (KCTP) actively promote bicycle tourism and even designed their

own eight-gear bicycle – the Ginrin—a high-performance, super-latively comfortable vehicle.

If ever there was a silver lining to a dark cloud, perhaps this apparent shift toward bicycles in Japan, at least as an option, will be one good thing to emerge from the March 11 disaster.

Practical Information

Bicycle Museum Cycle Center
18-2, Daisen Nakamachi, Sakai-ku
Sakai-shi, Osaka Prefecture, 590-0801
Tel: (072) 243-3196
www.h4.dion.ne.jp/~bikemuse/

Kyoto Cycling Tour Project (KCTP)
Kyoto Station Cycle Terminal
552-13 Higashi-Aburanokoji-cho
Aburanokoji-dori, Shiokoji-sagaru
Shimogyo-ku, Kyoto 600-8235
Tel: (075) 354-3636
www.kctp.net

CHAPTER 8

Dolls
Surrogates, Scapegoats, and Trusted Companions

A DECADE AGO IN THE BOSTON Children's Museum in Massachusetts, I came face to face with a doll named "Miss Kyoto Prefecture." She was one of 58 "Friendship Dolls" sent by Japan the United States in 1927. Elegantly crafted figures made with real human hair and dressed in *yuzen*-dyed kimono, individually they represented prefectures, the largest cities, colonial territories, and the imperial household. Collectively, they were Japan's gesture of reciprocity for the more than 12,000 blue-eyed dolls the United States had sent earlier the same year.

Through this exchange, Japan and the United States were able to diffuse mounting political tension. The two nations forged ties between their children that they themselves had difficulty making. Doll diplomacy served its purpose, though; it warmed young and old hearts alike on both sides of the Pacific. In Japan, the American dolls were distributed to primary schools and kindergartens while their Japanese counterparts found homes in children's museums and libraries across the United States. Miss Nagasaki went to New York, Miss Osaka to New Jersey, and Miss Nara settled in Idaho. But eventually, as doll expert Alan Scott Pate notes in his book *Ningyo: The Art of the Japanese Doll*, when relations broke down during the Pacific War, dolls on both sides became targets. They were defaced, put into storage or went missing.

The Friendship Dolls were made in a style known as *ichimatsu*, named after the handsome kabuki actor Sanogawa Ichimatsu. Popular during the Meiji era (1868-1912), they marked a change in Japan's image of "dolls" from an item for display to something to hold and play with. "Dolls in the past were offerings such as a prayer for a child's growth. But the role of the doll later shifted from a religious offering to a plaything," said Michio Takada of Tanaka-Ningyou Co. in Kyoto, an enterprise that has made dolls since 1573.

To get a better idea of the vast world of Japanese dolls, an excellent place to begin is Kyoto's Saga Doll Museum. Tucked away in a neighborhood studded with temples and even a few thatch-roofed houses, the museum possesses about 200,000 dolls mostly from the Edo period (1603-1867) and the Meiji era. The first floor has some magnificent *gosho ningyo* (palace dolls), chubby, bright white figures in bibs that were popular as gifts in the 17th and 18th centuries. Made of wood and coated with a gluey mixture of powdered oyster shells, the dolls are usually made to look like toddlers at play. The museum also has some excellent *karakuri ningyo* (mechanical dolls) known for their simple repetitive movements. This collection has a surprisingly smart-looking

Daikoku who lifts his mallet up and down while a circle of impish mice rotate around his feet.

Despite an immense and rich collection with rows upon rows of astounding dolls, the museum is not exhaustive in scope. You won't find modern day mass-produced hits. The Licca doll, for example, Japan's answer to Barbie—cuter, but a bit less curvaceous—is missing. Epoch Co.'s Sylvanian Families doll series, which features small furry animals complete with changeable clothes, houses and human furniture, also captivated children in Western countries, but is conspicuously absent.

However, one place where these fragments of cultural memory are not excluded is at Hokyoji temple in Kyoto. Known colloquially as the temple of dolls, for centuries Hokyoji served as a Zen convent for imperial princesses. When these royal women began their cloistered lives, they brought their dolls with them, and these precious figures now form the base of the temple's distinguished collection. Today, the temple accepts old, unwanted, or abandoned dolls dropped off by anyone. Head priest Eko Tanaka conducts a daily memorial service for the dolls until the temple's storage capacity is reached, at which point the dolls are taken away to be cremated in a mountaintop ceremony.

Although the temple is usually closed to the public, Hokyoji does come alive in March to celebrate the Doll Festival when the public may visit the doll collection. A temple employee explained to me that when people grow older, they often move into smaller houses and cannot keep the dolls they once proudly displayed in their homes. However, they feel they can't just throw them out either. "Why don't they give the dolls to their grandchildren?" I asked. "Children nowadays think these dolls are scary," she replied. "They don't want them, so their owners bring them here."

Seeing the dolls, I recalled a man I frequently saw in my old neighborhood near the Takanogawa river riding a bicycle with a doll seated in the front basket. On a few occasions, I even saw an elderly woman pushing a stroller that contained a baby doll rather than a real baby. A doll as a surrogate human is not as uncommon as I had thought at the time. Philosopher Rene Descartes (1596-1650) is said to have grieved so deeply at the death of his 5-year-old daughter Francine that he created a mechanical doll named after her and kept it with him at all times.

Contemporary attitudes toward dolls spurred my interest in visiting Tenshi no Sato, a museum devoted to the Super Dollfie doll. Super Dollfies—SDs—are ball-jointed dolls usually 60 centimeters (nearly 2 feet) in height that are made in Kyoto and sell for around ¥96,000. Volks Inc., the company that produces them, also owns the museum that has become a mecca for SD doll owners. Created for adult doll lovers, SDs have achieved a global fan base akin to that enjoyed by anime and cosplay. These dolls look like idealized versions of young adults and owners can customize them by choosing from a selection of eyes, hands, feet, hair and skin color.

On my way from the station, two women in front of me were wheeling small suitcases that turned out to contain their SDs. Upon entering the museum with my online reservation ticket, I was immediately impressed by the hushed, even reverent atmosphere. It became clear that Tenshi no Sato was actually much more than a museum; it was a shrine to dolls. In fact, to the right of the entrance is a life-size statue of the Virgin Mary cradling a SD. The first and fourth floors are reserved for adults to "play" with their dolls—no children are allowed in the museum—where play means dressing and positioning the dolls in order to photograph them. The second and third floors contain all the SD models produced since the doll was first created in 1999.

What is it about this doll that prompts people to make such an enormous investment in time and money? At Tenshi no Sato, people often spoke to others through their dolls, placing them together on a sofa or chair to take photos, or arranging them in positions mimicking that of friends or lovers. The SD seems to be the Friendship Doll of our times. They create opportunities for people who might otherwise find it difficult to communicate. If anything, dolls are accepting and dependable, qualities that inspire devotion, and that may be in short supply today. As the message above one of the display cases reads: "They will always be waiting for you at Tenshi-no-Sato."

Practical Information

Hokyoji temple
Teranouchi-dori Horikawa Higashi-iru
Kamigyo-ku, Kyoto 602-0072
Tel: (075) 451-1550
www.hokyoji.net/top.htm

Sagano Ningyo no Ie (Saga Doll Museum)
12 Saga-Toriimoto Busshodencho
Ukyo-ku, Kyoto 616-8434
Tel: (075) 882-1421
http://okatsuji.ac.jp/sagano/

Kuchuan Tenshi no Sato (Super Dollfie Doll Museum)
15 Saga-Tenryuji Wakamiyacho
Ukyo-ku, Kyoto 616-8371
Tel: (075) 982-3100
www.volks.co.jp

Tanaka-Ningyou Co. (Dollmaker/Store)
Higashiyama Sanjo-agaru
Sakyo-ku, Kyoto 590-0943
Tel: (075) 761-4151
www.tanaka-ningyo.co.jp

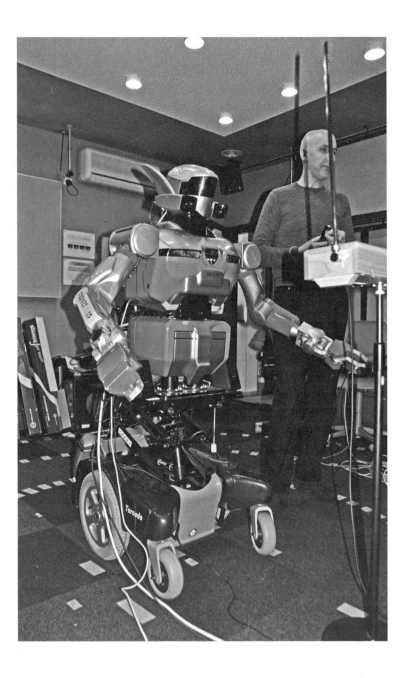

CHAPTER 9

Our Avatars, Ourselves
Robotic Innovation in Japan

Tᴇᴛsᴜᴊɪɴ 28-ɢᴏ, Tᴏʀᴀʏᴀɴ, Testsuwan Atom—Japanese robots are international celebrities. Honda Co's humanoid, Asimo, keeps a tight but versatile schedule. At a fundraiser a few years back, the white robot conducted the Detroit Symphony Orchestra in a rendition of "Impossible Dream." Three months ago, he blithely headed to Warsaw for an appearance at the annual Science Picnic. In the aftermath of the Great East Japan Earthquake he delighted children in the disaster-hit Tohoku region by dancing and kicking a soccer ball.

Other robots, such as Aibo, Sony's robo-dog—now a fixture in the Smithsonian's permanent collection—display neat fusions of the organic and the mechanical. Upon purchase, Aibo cannot walk, but gradually develops a repertoire of sounds and movements through interactions with humans. In short, the puppy grows up: it barks, responds to 100 spoken commands, shows anger by changing its eye color from green to red, and offers a conciliatory paw.

Sony phased out the adorable canine just seven years after its release, but other animal robots—some even cuter—have stepped in. Paro, the long-lashed, dark-eyed snow-white baby harp seal, seems to have secured a niche as a therapeutic companion for the elderly. Developed at the National Institute of Advanced Industrial Science and Technology by Takanori Shibata and covered with soft antibiotic fur, the 2.7-kilogram mechatronic seal is popular in care facilities across Japan, and increasingly in Europe and the United States since its release overseas in 2008. With five sensors, Paro responds to touch, light, sound, temperature and posture by moving its head, legs and tail to evoke primordial nurturing instincts in humans.

Paro has none of the hard surfaces characteristic of other would-be companion robots like, for example, Mitsubishi Heavy Industries' Wakamaru. Despite its extraordinary abilities to report news stories from the Internet, wirelessly contact family members or the hospital, and even offer reminders about daily medication, Wakamaru seems a distant presence in the home.

Now in its eighth generation, Paro's success does not derive from cuddly responsiveness and evocative cries alone. The real success may be that Paro is not meant to replace humans, but rather work in tandem with skilled caregivers. The willingness— or even desire—in Japan to coexist with mechanical beings is hardly explained by Shinto animism, often cited as the nation's cultural basis and the reason for its easy symbiosis with machines. Nor can the impact of post-war robot icon Astro Boy account for the aspirations of humans who would readily live in symbiance with machines.

The concept of modern robots in Japan was triggered in 1924 by Czech playwright Karel Capek's hit dram R.U.R. (Rossum's Universal Robots), which was staged in Tokyo two years after its Prague debut. Capek used the Czech term *robota*, meaning "serf labor", to refer to the synthetic, mass-produced factory workers in his play. Capable of feeling emotion, these robots soon revolted against their human inventors, and eventually killed them. However, such classic Frankenstein plots so pervasive in Western narratives lack resonance in Japan, a country where the bond between an artisan and his tools has deeper, enduring roots. Tools are revered in Japan not because they are "alive," but because they are an extension of the craftsman's body. Through daily use, a worker infuses his tools with his soul so that they acquire a kind of life of their own. This idea is common currency in Polynesia, where it is referred to as mana. Since a person and his tools make human livelihood possible, the product of his relationship is one of profound gratitude, a central value prevalent in Japanese culture that fosters a subjunctive mood. The tools are "as if" they are alive, but not mistaken for living things.

The impact of R.U.R. in Japan proved indelible, though the point of interest was not in the robotic revolution but rather the relationship between technology and humans. R.U.R. marks the beginning of a robot boom that has never waned. Like the swordsmith who folds steel thousands of times, infusing his spirit into what becomes the blade, robots in Japan were never conceived as enemies; they are friends and companions for life, tied intimately to humans in what anthropologists describe as fictive kinship.

Four years after the Tokyo performance of R.U.R., biologist Makoto Nishimura suggested building a *jinzo ningen* (artificial human, as robots were initially called in Japan), for the Grand Exposition in Commemoration of the Imperial Coronation in Kyoto in 1928. His creation was arguably Japan's first modern robot. Gakutensoku, meaning "learning of natural law," was more than 3 meters (nearly 10 feet) tall. He was dressed in a toga and sat on an ornate altar, with a mace in hand that lit up when he raised his wreathed head to the sky. Through rubber tubes and compressed air, his cheeks puffed as if he was actually breathing. Nishimura wanted to show that his robot was a part of nature. The *Osaka Mainichi Shimbun* quoted the biologist as saying, "If one considers humans as the children of nature, artificial humans created by the hand of man are thus nature's grandchildren." A phenomenal success, Gakutensoku went on tour to parts of Asia and Europe, just like many of his descendants have done.

Osamu Tezuka, father of Japanese animation and creator of

Tetsuwan Atom (Astro Boy), had read R.U.R. Yet ultimately he too created the image of friendly technology that helps men, women, and children. Tezuka formulated the Three Principles of Robot Law, and they echo those of renowned author Isaac Asimov's in his collection of nine short stories, *I, Robot*. Tezuka said that robots should never injure or kill humans; and that robots should serve humankind. But in his third law, Tezuka grants robots the right to live free and equal lives, which is a departure from Asimov's code, which says merely that robots should not destroy themselves.

Tezuka's generous granting of autonomy to robots is possibly because of a fundamental trust in tools and technology. Astro Boy, after all, symbolized an age when atomic power was seen as a symbol of hope for the future. The Expo '70 held in Osaka promoted the same narrative of robots as friendly, working machines. This view still thrives today in the world or roboticist Hiroshi Ishiguro of Osaka University. No one has tried more than Ishiguro to realized Tezuka's third law. Ishiguro builds androids that look like normal people. He uses silicone rubber and pneumatic actuators to create subtle movements such as breathing, twitching and blinking. For Ishiguro, if robots can "pass" as humans, they are likely to be accepted as counterparts in society, paving the way for surrogate selves, or what he calls geminoids.

July 2011 evidently marked a historical watershed in robot research in Japan. One of Ishiguro's androids made an appearance in a social setting, at Café Poco-Pen. Geminoid F, or Fumiko, as she is known, costarred the previous year in the 20-minute stage drama *Sayonara*, playing the role of an android. However, in this small café in Osaka, Fumiko assumed the role of hostess, albeit with certain restrictions due to a permanent sitting position and limited movements of the head, torso and arms. Controlled remotely by an unseen human operator with a microphone, the telepresence android took orders and conversed with customers. One of Ishiguro's biggest challenges with androids is to create *sonzaikan*, the sense of the presence of a person, not a human

impersonator or, at best, skillful ventriloquism.

Despite Japan's extraordinary expertise in robotics, the country was unprepared to use them in scenarios resulting from the March 11 Great East Japan Earthquake. Instead, iRobot's PackBot and Warrior from the United States assumed leading roles in missions. Although Quince, a Japanese robot for nuclear and biological disaster relief, was sent to the No. 2 reactor of the Fukushima No. 1 nuclear power plant to set up a gauge to measure contaminated water flooding the basement, it got caught on the staircase landing and failed to reach its destination, according to a Tokyo Electric Power Co. spokesperson.

The only useful Japanese robot appeared to be the Active Scope Camera, an 8-meter snakebot equipped with a fiber-optic camera that slithered along the ground and over rubble to relay images. According to Hiroshi Okuno, a professor who specializes in robotic audition at Kyoto University, the myth of nuclear safety has long stunted the development of rescue robots in Japan. Beyond research, the training of skilled operators of robots is essential. In fact, the Rescue Robot Contest began in 2001 with the idea to sharpen the public's sense of disaster preparedness and to train young people in the principles of rescue through remote-controlled robots they have designed themselves. Although many of the designs look like piles of junk on wheels, they are creative and require considerable skill to maneuver—skills that are ultimately transferable.

At the contest, rescuers sit at terminals out of view of an 8-meter rescue space. The aim is to rescue small cloth dummies quickly and gently. Fitted with sensors, these small figurines monitor the quality of a rescue. The Rescue Robot Contest is one way to combat complacency and take disaster preparedness to heart. Readiness is all.

Practical Information

Rescue Robot Contest
Osaka Electro-Communication University, Neyagawa Campus (sponsor)
18-8 Hatsucho, Neyagawa-shi, Osaka 572-8530
Tel: (072) 824-1131
www.rescue-robot-contest.org

PART III

A SENSE OF PLACE

CHAPTER 10

The Still Point
Authenticity Within an Evolving Cuisine

I N THE PAST TWO DECADES A NEW CULINARY PARADIGM—
molecular gastronomy—has attracted the devotion of chefs,
food critics, and diners worldwide. It's a movement that reflects
the flowering of a global scientific culture. Whether Tokyo or
Barcelona, the use of flash freezes, immersion blenders, *sous vide*
bags, and centrifuges has transformed the kitchen into a laboratory and cooking into a series of fantastic experiments. The
movement grew naturally out of the eclectic mode of *nouvelle
cuisine* that encouraged cross-cultural fusions and in the process
drew deeply from the Japanese culinary tradition. Elegant pre-
sentations, tiny portions, and a new emphasis on freshness, light-
ness, and unmasked flavors all represented some of the unique
contributions of Japan.

Japanese chefs in the U.S. have also long served as the conduits
and bridges of this thread of innovation. Matsuhisa Nobuyuki
redefined Japanese food for the American palate by creating a
Peruvian-Japanese fusion. While on a similar quest to please customers and satisfy his own creative spark, Masaharu Morimoto
has delighted in making visual cross-cultural puns. For instance,

in a dish called "Daikon Fettucine," served at his eponymous New York restaurant, Morimoto shaves the long white radish to mimic fettucine and dresses the mock-pasta in a tomato-basil sauce. Another, more radical, conduit of Japanese culinary practices—Michio Kushi—embarked on a lifetime crusade to promote macrobiotics, an extreme version of the traditional preference for impeccably fresh foods and seasonal-based ingredients.

In more recent years, Yoshiki Tsuji, the director of Japan's top culinary school—the Tsuji Culinary Institute in Osaka—opened the New York restaurant Brushstroke as a joint-venture with chefs from his own culinary academy in Osaka and chef David Bouley. The restaurant specializes in a modern interpretation of Japanese high-end cooking known as *kaiseki*. Steeped in a seasonal philosophy of foods and an accompanying aesthetic that strives for a near perfect balance of taste, texture and color, *kaiseki* originated in Kyoto as a meal to accompany a formal tea ceremony. At Brushstroke, Tsuji academy instructors prepare the food under the leadership of Chef Isao Yamada who learned his art from various master chefs in the Kansai area and worked at the prestigious Kitcho in Kyoto, perhaps the most esteemed among all *kaiseki* restaurants in Japan.

Yamada's *kaiseki*, designed to engage a modern transnational diner, illustrates the central paradox of all innovation: In order to transcend tradition it is first necessary to return to it. Or, know the rules before you break them. This return in the service of the future characterizes a particular historical moment today in Kyoto as well where a trend to rediscover traditional fare is now in full swing. The local tradition of Kyoto cuisine or *Kyo-ryori* comes in several genres. Besides the famed high-end *kaiseki*, it also includes *shojin* ryori or vegetarian temple cuisine, and *obanzai* or home cooking. But a major criterion for authenticity in any of the three now demands the use of *Kyo-yasai* or vegetables not only grown in Kyoto but that possess a historical continuity allowing them to be defined as "traditional" or "heirloom" vegetables.

The contrast suggested here is that the majority of vegetables eaten in Japan today are "aliens"—that is, introduced from abroad in two major waves. Between the fifth and twelfth centuries, Japan absorbed the turnip, giant radish, and taro from China and Korea. These vegetables, easy accompaniments with rice, have been thoroughly indigenized over the centuries and are now perceived as Japanese. The more recent or second wave came with the Western influence in the Meiji period (1868-1912) and includes the importation of tomatoes, green peppers, lettuce and cabbage. Hardy and often resistant to insect pests and blights they had an alleged competitive edge and after this native-newcomer encounter many traditional vegetables apparently disappeared.

According to Daizo Tanaka of the Kyoto Prefectural Agricultural Research Institute, vegetables grown within Kyoto Prefecture prior to the Meiji period can be labeled as "traditional." This includes 34 varieties among 17 species. Hardly a local phenomenon, the superior status granted to these vegetables is such that throughout Japan special sections in markets exist where they are sold as "*Kyo-yasai.*" In the quest for purity and authenticity, chefs of five-star traditional restaurants in Tokyo will typically source their vegetables directly from Kyoto. The country's capital for over 1,000 years, these Kyoto vegetables are esteemed for their distinct flavor and their symbolic national value.

Most of the *Kyo-yasai* are produced in Kamigamo, an area in the northwestern part of the Kyoto Valley and sold daily at auction near Kyoyasai Kanesho, a company that both promotes and distributes the vegetables. Shop owners and restaurateurs gather at the nearby vegetable market to bid on the freshest heirloom produce delivered by dozens of local farmers each day. Many of the vegetables have associations with particular temples and shrines since Kyoto has the most intense concentration of temples of anywhere in Japan. Long steeped in Buddhist ways of thinking that prohibited the consumption of meats, a vibrant vegetarian cuisine developed alongside the need for prodigious religious offerings of fresh produce.

I first heard of *Kyo-yasai* or Kyoto's heirloom vegetables from

the wife of the head priest of Anrakuji temple in my neighborhood in the eastern hills of Kyoto who had opened a small café
on the temple grounds where at lunchtime she served *Kyo-yasai*
and delicious coffee. Always enterprising, the Ito's had also invited
a farmer to sell his produce regularly just outside the temple gate
in the manner of other farmers who sell directly to consumers
around the city. One heirloom vegetable, the Shishigadani pumpkin, had a long association with the temple. Every year since 1790
on July 25, Anrakuji has held a memorial service for the lumpy
and plump hourglass shaped vegetable. Hundreds of guests visit
each year on the day to enjoy a pumpkin feast. Another temple-
affiliated vegetable is the feathery mibuna leaf associated with
Mibu temple. Other heirloom vegetables are popular but not
associated with religious institutions: the Kamo eggplant, the
Tango pear, the Horikawa burdock root, shrimp potato, the bright
red Kintoki carrot, and the chestnuts that hail from Tamba, the
same area prized for matsutake hunting during its brief fall gathering season.

Many of the *Kyo-yasai* can be found for sale at Nishiki, the
covered downtown market in central Kyoto. But a more intriguing way to encounter these prized vegetables is simply to wander
the back streets in the neighborhoods surrounding Nishiki where
many of them are arranged in baskets set on chairs or tables in
front of restaurants around lunchtime or before dinner. Besides
a nice respite from the ubiquitous plastic facsimiles of meals
found in restaurant windows on main streets across Japan, these
live vegetables advertise themselves and the freshness they represent. They boast the most ancient ethos of Japanese cuisine:
Eat local, fresh, and in season.

Kyoto vegetables are important part of Japan's culinary history
but they tell only part of the story. Being inland, Kyoto's location
far from the sea made access to fresh fish difficult. In the past,
much of the ocean fish would have been dried. But perhaps the
centerpiece of seafood was not even a fish at all but rather the
marvelously long leafed kelp (*kombu*) that grows in northern

waters off of Honshu and Hokkaido. With a deep olive-brown leaf, kelp is loaded with glutamates that act as a natural flavor intensifier. They are the quintessential source of *umami*, the fifth taste after sweet, sour, salty, and bitter. Discovered in the early twentieth century by Kikunae Ikeda, the chemist named the fifth taste after the word for "delicious" in Japanese.

That is largely the function of *umami*—it enhances other tastes and led to the discovery and commercial production of Monosodium Glutamate (MSG). Certain foods such asparagus, tomatoes, Parmesan cheese, meat, and kelp naturally carry glutamates, and the human tongue has special receptors that can sense them. The very core of Japanese cuisine rests on the *dashi* or clear soup stock made with kelp and dried bonito flakes that open a fine meal and set the tone for the evening.

Umami has been largely accepted worldwide since the 1980s as the fifth taste, and Chef Heston Blumenthal of England's famed restaurant—The Fat Duck—is an avid promoter of *kombu* and *dashi* because of the burst of *umami* they allow when mixed with other ingredients. He has adopted the broth as a taste fixer for jellies, risottos, soups, and stocks.

Basic *dashi* soup stock is made with spring water into which one piece of *konbu* is left to soak overnight. Then a boneless quarter of a dried bonito (that looks like a small apple-banana but hard and dark as real mahogany) is passed over what looks like a carpenter's plane attached to a hollow box. The fresh shavings fall into this box and when opening the small single drawer the shavings are pale pink and curly. They are simmered in the kelp water for no more than an instant. This forms just the base. Whatever else is placed inside—a cherrystone clam, a zest of citron, slender *enoki* mushrooms, or cubes of silken tofu, strive to preserve the intrinsic nature of each ingredient. The dish should conjure up of the rhythm of a certain season and the perennial tang of the ocean.

Practical Information

Tsuji Cooking Academy (one-time class)
1-3-17 Nishi-Tenman
Kita-ku, Osaka 530-0047
Tel: (06) 6367-1261
www.sanko.ac.jp/osaka-chori/
www.tsujicho.com/index.html

Uzuki Japanese Cooking
2-108 Uryuyama-cho, Kitashirakawa
Sakyo-ku, Kyoto 606-8271
Tel: Emi Hirayama (075) 711-2614
www.kyotouzuki.com

CHAPTER 11

Traveling The Coffee Road
Café Culture from Kaffa to Kyoto

B EAN, DRINK, DRUG AND RITUAL. More than the sum of its parts, coffee produces a distinct culture wherever people savor it. The trade routes forged through the passion for the roasted bean even rival the ancient silk routes that once linked vastly diverse cultures across Eurasia into a vital commercial and cultural network. While it is commonplace to speak of the "Silk Road," no one seems to mention a "Coffee Road" even though some of its segments would be equally ancient and the exchanges fostered just as indelible.

Originating sometime prior to 525 in the Ethiopian province of Kaffa (from which the beverage gets its name), coffee was first associated with Sufi monasteries as an aid for prayer and study. By the mid-15th century, coffee drinking had spiraled from Yemen up the Arabian Peninsula, leaving in its wake the world's first coffee plantations. Indeed, coffee always traveled in easy partnership with Islam. The world's earliest coffee houses opened in Mecca and from there spread throughout the Arab world.

Each culture along the Coffee Road left its signature on the drink. In Yemen, which held a global monopoly on coffee for hundreds of years, the roasting of coffee became a custom. The Yemenis traded the beans via the Red Sea port of Mocha (after which, centuries later, Americans would name their chocolate-flavored coffee). The Turks added spices such as clove, cinnamon, anise and cardamom. The Tunisians graced the beverage with orange-flower water, and West Africans added balsamic spices. With their usual panache, Moroccans added the potent aphrodisiac Spanish fly, dried rose petals and ambergris.

Whether a drug, a drink, or simply associated with "otherness," coffee was controversial in many quarters from the start. Vatican officials wanted it banned from Europe. After all, Christians drank wine but Muslims drank coffee. Had Pope Clement VIII shown himself unwilling to try the drink of the "infidels," the Coffee Road might have reached a dead end in Rome. But instead of condemnation, in 1600, the Pope declared it delicious and blessed the coffee. The Holy See's decision effectively threw open the gates to a vibrant new culture – the European coffee house.

Within the next 100 years, cafes sprung up all over Europe, starting in Venice. Given the delight in the stimulant and its lucrative trade potential, Europeans brought the coffee plant to their colonies in Indonesia and the Americas. Around this time, the Coffee Road took a surprising new turn and entered Japan through the back door. Dutch merchants of the Netherlands East India Company, confined to living on the small artificial island of Dejima off Nagasaki, were avid coffee drinkers. From 1641, knowledge of coffee began to trickle into Japan through this fan-shaped island.

Official policy restricted the communication with these "redheads" (as the Japanese called the Dutch) to traders, interpreters and prostitutes, who were in all likelihood the first Japanese to sample coffee. A document of the late 18th century lists some of the personal effects of a Nagasaki prostitute: a glass bottle, candles, a Dutch smoking pipe and a tin of coffee beans. But the honor of the earliest actual record of coffee consumption in Japan belongs to a doctor from Kyoto name Hirokawa Kai who traveled twice to Nagasaki in the late 1700s and lived there for a total of six years. Like other intellectuals of his time, the novelty of "Dutch learning" aroused the doctor's curiosity. As a physician, Horokawa was most interested in the medicinal value of coffee. He described the drip method, the use of milk and sugar (neither were part of the Japanese diet) and mixing the coffee with a knobby brownish mushroom for an optimal medicinal effect.

When the port of Kobe reopened for commercial trade in 1867, tea exporter Hokodo sent its ships from Kobe to the Philippines and other parts of Southeast Asia. They returned laden with coffee from India and served it to customers in their shop. Hokodo became the first public place in Japan to serve coffee. But full-blown coffee houses in Japan known as *kissaten* (literally, "tea-drinking shop") did not take off until the Taisho period, a time when over 13,000 Japanese immigrated to Brazil, where most worked in Sao Paolo on coffee plantations. The "*kissa*" of this period were serving much more than coffee; they conjured up glimpses of distant worlds that proliferated into a dizzying variety. "*Bijin kissa*" were coffee shops with gorgeous waitresses. The "*meikyoku kissa*" played only classical music masterpieces. The "jazz *kissa*" might have up to several thousand LPs. Most of the music *kissa* observed a no-talking rule.

Kyoto's oldest surviving *kissaten* date back to the early 1930s. Tsukiji, with its classical music, red velvet chairs and private nooks, was a haunt of novelist Junichiro Tanizaki. Salon de Thé Francois hung reproductions of Western masters on its walls, and Shinshindo (a no-music *kissa*) catered to students at nearby Kyoto University. The latter's founder had gone to France to learn how to make authentic French bread, but came back with a much larger vision. He took the lively Latin Quarter of Paris as his model. Shinshindo's huge slab tables, where it was possible to spend a day over a single cup of coffee, became a magnet for university students. These oak tables, made without nails by Living National Treasure Tatsuaki Kuroda, gave the place a hallowed ambience.

The halt on importing coffee during the war years put a

temporary damper on *kissaten* culture. Even then, necessity mothered some memorable inventions: coffee made from soybeans, potatoes or dandelion roots. Though tasting nothing like actual coffee, the ritual of making the beverage at least served to keep coffee's memory alive. The postwar years saw a revival of the *kissaten* offering again not only coffee but multiple themes. The *uta-goe* or sing-along *kissa* were coffee shops usually equipped with a piano, accordion and songbooks, with a director to lead the singing. Heady days these were, when Communism was fashionable and labor-movement, antiwar, but especially Russian folk songs enjoyed tremendous popularity. In the heyday of the 1960s, some *kissa* became highly specialized, so that it was possible to find "comic book *kissa*," "television *kissa*," ones that played only Beethoven or Mozart, or chanson, rockabilly, or even country and western. At least in Kyoto, one existed that focused entirely on the music of the Beatles' Ringo Starr.

Japanese *kissa* were vibrant social spheres, worlds apart from the *weltschmerz* characterized by poet T.S. Eliot's "Prufrock." Eliot had seen everything already and could only mutter in disillusionment, "I have measured out my life with coffee spoons." Japan's *kissa* were creative spaces. Kyoto's Honyarado served as the nucleus of the city's youth culture in the 1970s. Run collectively, built entirely by volunteer labor, it embraced a counter-culture ethos in which everyday life was to be artistic and education not the monopoly of schools. In light of this, teachers could be found anywhere, but perhaps especially in the *kissaten* where intellectuals, artists, and student activists gathered, as did foreign poets such as Alan Ginsberg, Kenneth Rexroth and Gary Snyder.

Not all *kissa* drew visionaries. Some catered to voluptuaries. The "no-pants *kissa*" were places where the waitresses wore no underpants. "Couples' *kissa*" provided privacy for romantic encounters—dim lights, high-back sofas all facing the same direction, and sometimes even curtains. The tremendous abundance and variety of public mingling places that the *kissa* represented was also symptomatic of cramped housing and family or work situations that made meeting in a *kissaten* a more comfortable option for business or pleasure. Technological innovation drove many *kissa* into obsolescence. All varieties of music *kissa* had thrived in an era when few individuals could afford imported records or expensive audio systems, and before the dawn of the karaoke box.

By the time Starbucks arrived in 1995, most of the *kissa* had already disappeared. The American megachain, now with 454 stores, is not the cause of the demise of the rich mosaic of *kissaten*; the first big challenge was the immensely successful chain Doutor Coffee, which opened in 1980 and now has over 1,000 shops nationwide. Doutor not only drove the price of coffee down by at least 200 yen, but also offered a novel set of traits—speed and efficiency with quality. Starbucks took this a step further with wi-fi, power outlets and a completely non-smoking environment.

But coffee is more than a drink in Japan. It is also a

performance. Watch a coffee meister in the act of preparing siphon coffee: The alcohol lamp heats the water in the lower glass chamber while the vapor pressure drives it up a glass tube and into the upper dome. With perfect timing, the meister stirs and stirs the mixture with uncommon finesse. Through him, we are transported back in time to those first Whirling Dervishes who graciously gave us coffee.

Practical Information

UCC Coffee Museum
6-6-2, Minatojima-Nakamachi
Chuo-ku, Kobe 650-0046
Tel: (078) 302-8880

Tsukiji
Shijo-Kawaramachi agaru, Higashi-iru
Nagakyoku, Kyoto 604-8026
Tel: (075) 221-1053

Salon de Thé Francois
Nishikiyamachi-dori, Shijo-sagaru
Shimogyo-ku, Kyoto 600-8019
Tel: (075) 351-4042

Hanafusa
Residence Okazaki 1st Fl, 43-5 Higashi Ten'ocho
Sakyo-ku, Kyoto 606-8332
(075) 751-9610

Shinshindo
88 Oiwakecho Kitashirakawa
Sakyo-ku, Kyoto 606-8224
Tel: (075) 701-4121

Elephant Factory
HK Building, 2nd Fl, 309-4 Bizenjimacho
Kiyamachi Higashi-iru, Takoyakushi-dori
Nakagyo-ku, Kyoto 604-8023
Tel: (075) 212-1808

Café Honyarado
229 Oharaguchicho
Kamigyo-ku, Kyoto 604-8015
Tel: (075) 222-1574

Evian Coffee
1-7-2 Motomachi-dori
Chuo-ku, Kobe 650-0022
Tel: (078) 331-3265

CHAPTER 12

Traces of China in Japan

T HE YEAR 2011 WAS CHINA'S JADE YEAR as the country celebrated the 100th anniversary of its 1911 revolution, when nationalist forces brought down the country's last imperial dynasty—the Qing—and established the Republic of China. Both China and Taiwan consider themselves heirs to that government, and celebrate the pivotal event according to their own visions of history. Though they may disagree on many points, they converge enthusiastically one: a reverence for Sun Yatsen (1866-1925) as the father of the revolution who ushered in a modern China.

On the increasingly swanky Sanjo-dori street in Kyoto, not far from the China Café that serves "Oolong coffee," the MOVIX Cinema was showing the film *1911* to coincide roughly with the month the rebellion occurred 100 years ago. The film tells the story of the resentment of the majority Han Chinese toward the ruling Manchu minority and the bloody road to a republic. It features Hong Kong's multi-tasking artist Jackie Chan as co-director and star in a movie packed with action scenes and a catalogue of historical figures that for the uninitiated requires footnotes. Chan plays Huang Xing, Sun Yatsen's deputy, one of the founders of the

Kuomintang and the revolution's military leader.

Watching the film in Japan lends a sharp edge to the story. After all, in 1644 when the Manchus invaded China and first established the Qing dynasty, Ming loyalists fled to Japan, where the Tokugawa shogunate gave them sanctuary in Nagasaki. Both shogunate and the loyalists, convinced that China was in the corrupting hands of foreigners, viewed Japan as the potential heir of Chinese Confucian civilization. Indeed, for Japan until the modern era China had always embodied the highest values of civilization.

These values were transmitted by merchants, Buddhist monk-scholars, and recent expatriate loyalists to the Ming dynasty, an elite group that included calligraphers, doctors of Chinese medicine, musicians and literati. The presence of these foreigners attracted Japanese and other intellectuals from afar on spiritual and intellectual pilgrimages to Nagasaki to learn from these representatives of mainland civilization. One such figure was the Chinese monk Yinyuan Longqu (1592-1673), or Ingen Ryuki in Japanese, a high-ranking Rinzai Zen priest in China who came to Japan in 1654. Ingen's encounter with his own Buddhist sect in Japan, seemingly unchanged since its introduction in the late 12th century, caused him some dismay.

Japanese Rinzai appeared to be suspended in time, untouched by the many doctrinal changes that had occurred in the meantime to Rinzai in China during the late Ming period (1368-1644). The discrepancies were great enough to prompt Ingen to venture to Edo (present-day Tokyo) for an audience with Tokugawa Ietsuna (1641-1680), who ultimately allowed him not only to establish an independent sect but granted the priest land in Uji, south of Kyoto, to build a temple.

Ingen named the newly reformed Rinzai sect—the Obaku sect—after the cork tree-covered mountain where his home temple stood in China, and Manpukuji temple, the Japanese rendition of his former temple's name. Besides a new form of Buddhism, Ingen introduced new foods and culinary practices to Japan.

Watermelon, lotus root, and kidney beans are all accredited to Ingen. According to Shikyoku Araki, director of education at Manpukuji, the strictly vegetarian cuisine for which the temple is now famous—*fucha ryori*, or "food to accompany tea"—originated in temple offerings shared by priests after major religious rituals. A crucial aspect of Obaku ritual was the drinking of *sencha*, a general term for steeped leaf tea.

Leaf Tea Introduced

The drinking of leaf tea was first imported to Japan in the late 16th century, though not widely consumed in the country until the mid-18th century. By Ming times, Zen temples in China had stopped using the powdered tea of *chanoyu* that had gained converts among the upper classes. Having assumed the status-marker of Japanese identity, *chanoyu* (*chado*) has largely eclipsed *senchado* or the Chinese tea ceremony in contemporary Japan.

According to Sessho Doi, fifth head of the Higashi Abe lineage of *senchado*, more than 100 different schools of the Chinese tea ceremony are active in Japan today. Practitioners use a small pot and five tiny cups to serve multiple guests. The preferred tea is the bright jade-green colored leaf tea of *gyokuro* known for its fragrance and full-bodied flavor that leaves a strong aftertaste. Says Hiroaki Mizuki of Ippodo, Kyoto's classic tea purveyor, the pale green tea is meant to be "sipped slowly and savored on the tongue."

Chinese Community Thriving

A new China is thriving in Japan today whose residents continue to serve as a major leaven in Japanese society both inside and outside the older communities where they originally settled. Japan's three best-known Chinatowns—in Nagasaki, Yokohama and Kobe—all opened in the 19th century and drew immigrants mostly from provinces along the coast of China: Guangdong (especially from Guangzhou) and Fujian, as well as Sanjiang—a collective term for the three eastern provinces of Jiangsu, Zhejiang and Jiangxi. Thus, during the Meiji era (1868-1912) Cantonese was the most widely spoken dialect among Chinese residents in Japan. Typical of the times, the Chinese of this epoch identified with their home provinces rather than a nation. For example, the Shanghainese associated themselves solely with the Shanghai area.

One of the most important institutions for fostering the continuity of heritage among overseas Chinese in Kobe is the Kobe Tongwen Chinese School. Established in 1899 with primary and middle schools, it is one of the largest overseas Chinese schools in the world and has long served as the center of education for Chinese in the Kansai region. Initially, Cantonese served as the language of instruction but the school switched to Mandarin (the official language of China) during the Sino-Japanese War (1937-1945), a move that ultimately led to Mandarin becoming the common language of that Chinatown.

Not far from the school is Kobe's Chinatown known as Nankinmachi. Small in comparison to Yokohama's Chinatown, it

remains a lively enclave of over 100 restaurants and outdoor food vendors. But for upscale Chinese cuisine, one of Kobe's most traditional restaurants—the elegant Totenkaku—is found in Kitano, a neighborhood of residences built by wealthy foreigners who settled there in the late 19th century. Located inside a century-old mansion—the F. Bishop House—the Totenkaku has high ceilings, plush carpets, exquisite Chinese artifacts and luxurious draperies. The restaurant specializes in Peking duck flown in from China and has an array of floral teas served in transparent pots that blossom into veritable underwater gardens.

If these tastes of China in Japan only serve to whet a more substantial appetite, the port of Kobe has a weekly ferry to China: In two days, you can be in Shanghai.

Practical Information

Obakusan Manpukuji temple (for Fucha cuisine, reservations one week ahead)
34 Sanbanwari, Gokanosho
Uji, Kyoto 611-0011
Tel: 0774) 32-3900
www.obakusan.or.jp

The Sencha Tea Ceremony Association of Japan
(Manpukuji at the Senchado Kaikan)
Tel: (0774) 32-1368
www.senchado.com

Ippodo
(Main Store Kyoto)
Teramachi-dori Nijo
Nakagyo-ku, Kyoto 604-0915
(075) 211-3421
www.ippodo-tea.co.jp

Totenkaku Royal Chinese Restaurant
3-14-18 Yamamoto-dori
Chuo-ku, Kobe 650-0003
Tel: (078) 231-1351
www.totenkaku.com

Japan China International Ferry Co.
San-Ai Bldg, 2 Fl., 1-8-6 Shinmachi
Nishi-ku, Osaka 550-0013
Tel: (06) 6536-6541
www.shinganjin.com

Footbath at the Arashiyama Keifuku Station, Kyoto

Top Left: Fortunes appear when paper touches water at Kifune Shrine in Kyoto.

Top Right: Beauty-enhancing waters at Yasaka Shrine, Kyoto

Above: Bamboo grove found at Arashiyama, Kyoto, Japan (Photo by Wai Chung Tang)

Opposite: Waterway in Kyoto

Top Left: Bamboo lanterns for Kyoto Higashiyama Hanatouro at Maruyama Park at sunset (Photo by Liyi Lee)

Top Right: At Toji Temple in Kyoto, a classic Japanese purification fountain (Photo by Pargastone)

Above: Iwashimizu Hachimangu shrine's bamboo ema with Edison's portrait

Top: Kareki Shrine, Awajishima, Hyogo Prefecture, where a piece of aloeswood is enshrined

Above: Carved wall panel at Kobe's Nankinmachi

Top: Torii gate on Lake Biwa (Photo by Fatalsweet)

Above: A typical means of travel in Kyoto, bicycles are often fashion statements.

Top: Participant in the annual Rescue Robot Contest, Kobe (Courtesy of Yasuhiro Masutani)

Above: Guardian robot of Kobe—Tetsujin 28-go (Gigantor)— erected four years after the 1995 Great Hanshin Earthquake as a symbol of the city's revival, Wakamatsu Park in Kobe

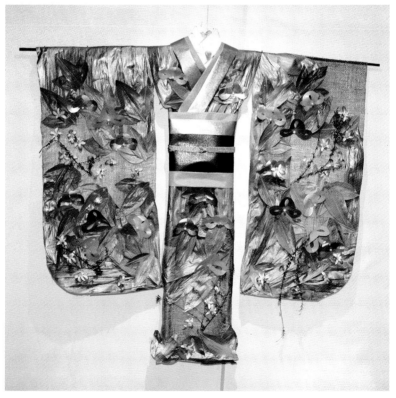

Top Left: Kimono fashion on display (Photo by Lucian Milasan)
Top Right: Young Japanese women in kimono on Coming of Age Day (Photo by Wdeon)
Above: Traditional Japanese kimono dress on display (Photo by Khwi)

Young woman models kimono in Kyoto.

Below: Sending dolls off to sea at Awashima Shrine, Kada, Wakayama during the Doll Festival on March 3

Bottom: Super Dolfies getting acquainted at the Super Dolfie Museum, Kyoto

Opposite: Memorial for cremated dolls at Hokyoji temple, Kyoto

Top: Kobe Port Tower and Maritime Museum stand as symbols of prosperity in Meriken Park in Kobe. (Photo by Sean Pavone)

Above: Japan's Bullet Train makes a brief stop in Kyoto. The Tokkaido Shinkansen is the world's busiest high-speed rail line carrying 151 million passengers annually. (Photo by Sean Pavone)

Opposite: Kansai International Airport interior detail, a section of the Void (Photo by Siraanamwong)

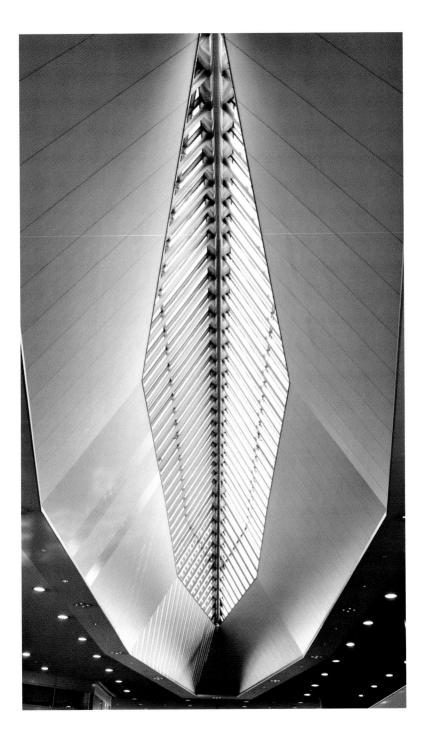

明治時代
Meiji period

Top: Crazy Dragon billboard on Dotonbori Street in Osaka (Photo by Siraanamwong)

Above Left: Carp decoration atop the roof of Himeji Castle, Himeji City in Honshu during the Meiji era (1868-1912) (Photo by Xian Hui Serene Ho)

Above Right: The octopus is the mascot of the Dotonbori Konamon Museum—a place devoted to the art and history of flour-based foods. (Photo by Natulia Pushchina)

The New World in Osaka. The neighborhood was created
in 1912 with New York and Paris serving as models.
(Photo by Sean Pavone)

Top: Visitors feed wild deer in Nara. (Photo by Tupungato)

Above: A monk asks for alms by the fountain outside Nara Station on the Kentetsu line. (Photo by Wai Chung Tang)

Top: The approach to the Shinto shrine Kibune Jinja, Kyoto
(Photo by Sivanon)

Above: Torii gate to Jishu-jinja, a Shinto shrine located within
the compound of Kiyomizu-dera (Kiyomizu temple) in Kyoto.
The shrine is dedicated to love and matchmaking.
(Photo by Xian Hui Serene Ho)

Top: Fish-shaped gong at Manpukuji Obaku-Zen temple in Uji, Kyoto

Above: Crossing tsurugi during waraku practice in Kyoto (Photo by John Einarsen)

Opposite Top: Central pulse of Nankinmachi, Kobe's Chinatown

Opposite: Nankin-Machi in Kobe is one of only three designated Chinatowns in Japan. Like many Chinatowns, the area is a tourist attraction. (Photo by Sean Pavone)

Top Left: The Gion Matsuri, one of Japan's oldest and most famous festivals, is celebrated throughout the month of July. (Photo by Chiharu)

Top Right: Golden portable shrine at Osaka's Tenjin, Matsuri, a festival that has been taking place annually for a thousand years (Photo by Ivan Cheung)

Above: Lantern float for the Nebuta Matsuri is on display at the Warasse Nebuta Museum in Aomori. (Photo by PKOM)

Opposite: Ima-Tenko + Kiraza, Kyoto (Photo by Hiroshi Mimura)

Top: Hideki Kimura's "Gorillas' Daily Life" at the Kyoto City Zoo

Above: Hideki Kimura's Tigers in the Kurochiku Building, Kyoto

Opposite: Stained-glass silk scarf by Issey Miyake

Top Left: Cosplay of Toudou Heisuke from the video game series Hakuouki Shinsengumi Kitan (Photo by maho)

Top Right: Watercolor of Kagamine Len by Yu Tsukinaga (Photo by maho)

Above: Cosplay of vocaloid Kagamine Len, Yumemirukotori, second in a series by Crypton Future Media (Photo by maho)

Opposite: Sweet Lolitas from Kyoto (Photo by Kazuhiko Susukida)

Top: Osaka's famous Dotonbori Street. The Glico Man is a local icon.
(Photo by Siraanamwong)

Above: Japanese women wear kimono for viewing at Kiyomizu temple in Kyoto.
(Photo by PKOM)

Top: Maneki neko beckons passersby to try the the lottery, Kyoto.

Above: Interior of Maishima Water Treatment Plant designed by Hundertwasser, Osaka

Top: Torii gates at Fushimi-inari Shrine, Kyoto. These gates line the hillsides that lead up to the main shrines at the top of the hill. (Photo by Christopher Rawlins)

Above: Dry rock garden depicting islands and sea at Nanzenji temple, Kyoto

Opposite: A traditional Buddhist rock garden In Koya-san, Japan, with colorful leaves and a blue sky in the background (Photo by Xerion)

Above: Osaka Castle during Sakura season
(Photo by Ukiyoe)

Top: The Buddhist Temple Rokuon-ji, more commonly known as Kinkaku-ji (the Temple of the Golden Pavilion), Kyoto (Photo by Fg2)

Above: Zen Garden at Ryōan-ji Temple in Kyoto (Photo by Cquest)

Japanese bathroom with washlet toilet by
TOTO Ltd. (Photo Courtesy of TOTO Ltd.)

CHAPTER 13

Geography as Destiny
Crafting Islands in Japan

ARTIFICIAL ISLANDS HAVE A WAY of conjuring up mythical locales, such as Avalon or Laputa, together with floating cities of the sort that futuristic architects Buckminster Fuller and Kenzo Tange had in mind. For the past 50 years, technological and engineering achievements have made manmade islands in Japan an option as urban sprawl has largely triggered their proliferation. Osaka Bay now has eight artificial islands and 95 percent of its 160-kilometer shoreline is reclaimed land. While the form and function of artificial islands in recent decades revolve around habitation, industry, disposal and airports, Japan has a long history of crafting islands for a variety of other purposes.

The *Nihon Shoki* describes how the 33rd ruler of Japan—Empress Suiko—employed Korean artisans to build a garden that would feature a miniature version of the island-mountain Sumeru of Buddhist cosmology. While the Empress's commission surely expressed her exemplary faith, a type of garden known as the "Pure Land Garden" later became fashionable during the Heian period. Through a technique known a *shukkei* or "contracted scenery" (not to be confused with *shakkei, "*borrowed scenery")

gardens were crafted to replicate actual or imagined landscapes. In the case of Pure Land Gardens, a scene glimpsed through a description in a sutra or a painting might serve as a template.

Byodoin temple's graceful Phoenix Hall (depicted on the back of the ¥10 coin) in Uji, Kyoto Prefecture, is located in one of the few gardens remaining in that style. It is on the artificial island of Nakajima, which was built up and broadened with stones from a "seed" islet in the midst of a mirror-like pond. The Hall is meant to represent Amitabha Buddha's palace in the Western Paradise as described in the Infinite Life Sutra. Symbolic islands such as this one are visual aids for a living faith and serve to draw the remote near and allow the viewer to become more intimate with the transcendent.

Ancient gardens of the Asuka and Nara periods (538-794 AD)—which often employed *shukkei*—were even called *shima* (island) rather than *niwa* (garden) for their preference to represent seascapes and island scenery. Such windswept islands and rocky beaches were later canonized in the Edo period (1615-1868) through the work of Confucian scholar Hayashi Junsai, who traveled the entire archipelago appraising its scenery. His assessment crystallized into tradition. These *sankei* or "three most spectacular scenic spots" in Japan—Matsushima, Miyajima, and Amanohashidate—all depict various kinds of islands, from pine clad islets to sandbars immortalized over the centuries in poems, paintings, and certainly incorporated into the grammar of gardens.

But beauty and religious contemplation were never the only motivations for artificial island construction in the premodern period. Japan built islands for defensive purposes that included the concept of cultural quarantine. The small—fan-shaped island of Dejima in Nagasaki Bay, originally a peninsula, got its shape when a canal was dug through the landmass. Built during Japan's period of national isolation, the purpose of this micro-island was to restrict the inflows and outflows of people and information. The only foreigners then allowed in Japan (a handful of Dutch and Chinese traders) were confined to Dejima. The island has since disappeared. Postwar urban spread in Nagasaki engulfed most of the former island. That which remained of Dejima was dredged to widen the river.

Daiba, too, was an artificial island of defense, though explicitly so with its cannons. In the late Edo period, the Tokugawa shogunate ordered the construction of a series of artificial island fortresses in Tokyo Bay equipped with artillery to protect Japan from foreign attacks that the government feared after its encounter with Commodore Perry and his formidable Black Ships. By the mid-Meiji era, these islands were no longer necessary. Four were removed to allow for smooth ship passage and just two remain today though transformed into leisure and residential areas.

Japan's admiration for islands, whether viewing them or crafting them, reflects its own geography as much as pays tribute to its dependence on the sea. Throughout the 1960s, the Japanese avant-garde architectural movement known as "Metabolism" profoundly influenced the ideas of urban space and architecture in Japan. Metabolist proposals for floating cities drew global attention that coincided with the accelerated development of the sea and sea-front along Osaka Bay. What transpired in the following decades seems an attempt to bring some of these ideas to fruition.

Central to the Metabolists' project was the ocean as the site of a new civilization. They rebelled against Modernism on the grounds that it lacked life, for architecture was to be a dynamic process receptive to change. Respect for ecology, symbiosis of styles, and sustainability were all part of their credo. Osaka-born Tange envisioned a series of ocean cities along the entire Pacific coast that would launch a new era of "Marine Civilization." This new emphasis on the sea, a kind of "blue revolution" would finally free humankind from 5,000 years of tyranny by continent-based civilization. The vast oceans that covered three-quarters of the planet, viewed as a new frontier, would make it possible to transfer the congested population offshore.

The city of Osaka has four offshore artificial islands: Sakishima, Yumeshima, Maishima and Phoenix Island. Sakishima is the only one of the group built for human habitation; the others are related to waste disposal. The island center—known as Port Town—filled with condominium high-rises, has a population of 26,000. Through the center of town flows an artificial river. A variety of mushrooms now grow in the soil and on trees. In the 30 years since its completion, the vegetation has become luxuriant, a tribute to the persistence of life. The expression "trash-island" used to describe Sakishima often leads to a common misunderstanding that the island is somehow made up of cartons, bottles, old bicycles, and car wrecks. But the foundation of this island is a mixture of fine and gravely ash, essentially what remains after incinerating huge quantities of garbage.

The whole process of incineration can be witnessed on neighboring Maishima. From the Osaka mainland, the Maishima Incinerator and Water Treatment Plants look like something out of the Arabian Nights. The two minarets crowned with golden onion domes are actually the chimneys of the two plants. The incinerator handles 900 tons of trash per day from just two districts in Osaka.

Maverick Viennese architect Friedensreich Hundertwasser designed the exterior of these buildings. While not a Metabolist per se, Hundertwasser shared many of the movement's ideas, especially its insistence on organic design and its criticism of Modernist sterility. He ranted against "window apartheid," the compulsion not to mix windows of different shapes and sizes in the same building. Not only was utilitarian and functional architecture uninhabitable, but it was immoral by his standards. Since straight lines and identical objects do not exist in nature, Hundertwasser incorporated curved lines into his shapes by crowning rooftops with trees, placing planters against walls, and adding uneven floors and nonlinear tables.

If what humans most yearn for in their lives is variety and beauty harmonious with nature, Hundertwasser gave it to us in this building. The Maishima Incinerator is a boldly life-affirming structure from an artist with a buoyant spirit bent on creating happy habitats wherever humans happen to live and work.

Whether natural or artificial, the fascination for islands is a persistent motif throughout Japanese history. In antiquity, such islands were refuges for contemplation. In recent times, there is an actual attempt to inhabit artificial ones, and dream of oceanic utopias.

Practical Information

Maishima Incinerator Plant (Reservations required)
1-2-48 Hokko Shiratsu
Konohana-ku, Osaka 554-0041
Tel: (06) 6630-3353

Byodoin temple
116 Renge, Uji
Uji-shi, Kyoto 611-0021
Tel: (0774) 21-2861
www.byodoin.or.jp

PART IV

THE ARTS

Butoh
Theater of the Soul

UTOH IS PART OF A GROWING JAPANESE DANCE lineage often described as "avant-garde," although it has been around for half a century and is now well established not only in Japan, but in the Americas, Europe, Asia, and Oceania. The year 2005 saw the opening of the International Butoh Academy in Palermo, Sicily, but the form will probably continue to be regarded as experimental as long as the spirit of transgression that marked its beginnings still inspires the dance.

The word butoh means "dance" in Japanese, but it came to be used more narrowly in the mid-19th century to refer specifically to recently imported Western dance forms that were fashionable at that time, including ballet, the foxtrot, and the tango. In the late 1950s, when Hijikata Tatsumi (1928-1986) started his avant-garde dance movement in Tokyo, he adopted the word "butoh" to distinguish the new forms from native Japanese dance traditions found in kabuki and noh. At the same time, he wanted to distance butoh from the light or bright aspect of these imported Western dances, so he added the word *ankoku*, meaning "deep darkness," to make ankoku butoh or "dance of utter darkness."

The aesthetic of ankoku butoh first developed in the post-World War Two years, a time characterized by tremendous social change in Japan. The atomic bombs exploded over Hiroshima and Nagasaki had revealed that the impossible—utter annihilation—was now possible. The juggernaut of American culture was fast transforming Japanese institutions and lifestyles, and threatening to efface or at least muddle Japan's own heritage. There was a pervasive sense of urgency across fields to resurrect an authentic Japanese identity. It found expression in several kinds of protest. One of these was in the field of ethnography and folklore studies. The works of Yanagita Kunio (1875-1962) and Origuchi Shinobu (1887-1957), which celebrated the rural and marginal, enjoyed widespread popularity. These researchers had gathered stories and local customs throughout Japan that could be used to foster a new sense of traditional identity, and highlighted the country's great regional diversity. Another form of protest characteristic of the era was found in the political sphere. The ANPO protests were massive attempts to challenge the renewal of the Japan-U.S. Security Treaty that granted the American government use of military bases throughout Japan.

In dance, butoh represented yet another idiom of protest. It emerged in response to Japan's rupture with the past and the bitter irony of becoming modern and on the road to economic ascendancy without a coherent identity to accompany it. Butoh conjured up body postures evocative of the past and returned to the darkened pre-modern stage that had characterized kabuki and noh before the advent of electrical illumination had "vulgarized" the theater. These techniques of "return" revealed the presence of nostalgia at the heart of butoh. The tangible proof of this sentiment became the kimono shreds worn by some dancers that reiterated the fragmentation of Japanese identity. But butoh's nostalgia was ultimately not limited to national boundaries, since its protest was against modernity itself. For this reason an appropriate response could not be a simple return to earlier Japanese theatrical forms. Butoh sought models of transgression, not regression. In their quest, influential dancers looked to Europe for these models, since they recognized that people elsewhere had also been reacting to modernity and the loss of vital parts of the self.

While deeply rooted in Japan, butoh was a robust product of cross-fertilization. It drew from Surrealism, a movement that cultivated the exploration of fantasies, dreams, and the investigation of the subconscious mind that Freud had pioneered from his couch in Vienna. Prior to forging the butoh aesthetic, Hijikata and Ohno Kazuo (1906-2010), the form's co-founder, had studied ballet, German modern dance, and had also been influenced by French mime. Ohno was taught by Eiguchi Takaya, who had gone to Germany to study with Mary Wigman, one of the great pioneers of German Expressionist dance. Ohno also learned techniques from Ishii Baku, a pioneer of Western modern dance in Japan and an important student of Giovanni Rossi, who had been hired by the Japanese Imperial Theater to teach classical dance and modern ballet. However, Ohno's actual "calling" as a dancer came while watching the renowned flamenco artist Antonia Mercé (known as "La Argentina") in Tokyo. Stunned by her performance, Ohno decided on the spot to devote himself to dance. Hijikata, on the other hand, drew inspiration from Western literature. Among his favorite writers were Jean Genet, the Marquis de Sade, Georges Bataille, and Edgar Allan Poe.

Butoh was eminently capable of producing evocative dreamscapes as evidenced in the first performance staged in Tokyo in 1959. Called *Kinjiki* (Forbidden Colors), based on Mishima Yukio's novel of the same title. The work dealt with a homoerotic theme and included the strangling of a live chicken on stage over the crotch of a boy. It concluded with the man in pursuit of the boy on a completely darkened stage with only the sounds of running and heavy breathing. According to butoh legend, this shocking performance resulted in half the audience leaving the theater.

From the start then, Hijikata's ankoku butoh attempted to shatter the complacency of his spectators by placing on stage everything that our modern world required to be hidden from sight because it caused existential discomfort—disease, disability, sexuality, death, and the waste produced by massive material consumption. Whether physically buried in the earth or repressed deep in the human psyche, these banished parts became phantoms that he believed haunted the souls of modern people. By putting these taboos onto the stage, Hijikata urged people to look at these disowned remnants of themselves.

To Hijikata's dark and powerful charisma, Ohno provided a striking contrast. He brought to the dance the qualities of illumination and tenderness. Through 20 years of collaboration, the two men formed what might be thought of as the yin and yang that constitute the totality of butoh. Incidentally, Ohno and Hijikata were both from northern Japan. In Hijikata's case, he had experienced great poverty there. His sister, who had been sold into prostitution so that the family could survive, haunted the dancer his entire life. What became one of butoh's most typical postures—a bow-legged crouch—was the familiar stance both men had often seen of farmers consumed by hunger and permanently stooped from cropping rice in the fields. Along with this posture were others: slumped, bow-legged, and pigeon-toed. Hijikata initially tried to recapture the pre-modern Japanese body considered more in tune with the rhythms of nature. He believed that by reliving certain postures, the memories encapsulated in them could be reactivated not only in the dancer, but also create a resonance with the audience. Ultimately, they went beyond being emblems of the rigors and sheer physicality of pre-modern life in Japan, and became attempts to return to a pre-socialized body emptied of habitual movement and therefore open to new creative forms of expression.

Given its deeply internal orientation, butoh training avoids the use of mirrors in the studio that would distract from practices intended to induce interior transformation. Dancers learn techniques designed to deconstruct the modern body conditioned by mechanical time and on whose scaffolding they see the construction of an illusory modern self. Butoh can be thought of as dipping into the past in order to engage in a subtle conversation or negotiation with tradition. It shares something with the Japanese Buddhist aspiration for *satori*—that integrating flash attained when a person comes to the end of logic's tether.

The ankoku butoh of the 1960s was an underground dance performed in small theaters in Tokyo. By the 1970s, butoh had come into its own as a robust and creative dance that resonated with wider currents of nostalgia for the rural and marginal as introduced by Yanagita and Origuchi. By the 1980s, butoh enjoyed an international presence, especially in Europe. Since the 1990s, indigenous butoh has sprung up in many parts of the world. These new non-Japanese butoh currents are challenging the definition of the form as a Japanese dance made exclusively for a Japanese body.

Although Hijikata passed away in 1986, Ohno performed his last dance in 2007 at the age of 100. He danced from a wheelchair taking great care in the perfection of his hand movements. Since there is no ideal body type in a genre such as butoh, where dance can only emerge from a deep knowledge of whatever body a person has been given in this life, it follows that there is also no retirement age in butoh. Today, the largest butoh company in Japan is Dairakudakan, but another important company—Sankaijuku—still works out of Paris. Carlotta Ikeda has also lived in France since 1978 with her all-female company Ariadone. Renowned dancers such as Pina Bausch (1940-2009) in Germany had encountered butoh performers in Paris as early as the 1970s. Therefore, butoh and Bausch mutually influenced each other at an early stage while both drew from a common source—German Expressionistic dance. Today, there are many varieties of butoh. Some are extravagant and stylized spectacle, while others are more like Jerzy Grotowski's (1933-1999) "Poor Theatre," with the exterior elements of costume and scenery stripped away in order to focus on the actors' ability to create transformations through the perfection of the craft alone. The core of such performance is the encounter between the spectator and performer.

One dramatist admired by Hijikata was the Frenchman Antonin Artaud (1896-1948), who advocated an end to what he called the "artistic dallying with forms." Instead, Artaud said that performers should be like "victims burnt at the stake, signaling through the flames." Having witnessed kabuki during his artistic training, Artaud remarked: "The Japanese are our masters." Unfortunately, he did not live to see the birth of butoh, which comes nearest to his own theatrical ideal. While butoh is usually referred to as "dance," it is better understood as kind of theater—a theater of the soul. When it is performed sensitively, it is like an exorcism that allows the demons within us to flow out. It combines what Artaud refers to as the "fiery magnetism of image" with "spiritual therapeutics." Above all, it enlivens the human capacity for astonishment.

Practical Information

Ima-Tenko Butoh Studio
Butoh Company Ima-Tenko+Kirazu
13-1 Ugabecho, Higashikujo
Minamiku, Kyoto 601-8021
Tel: (075) 748-6778
www.ima-tenko.com

CHAPTER 15

Arms of Peace
Japan's Newest Martial Art Goes to Rome

R OME HAS ALWAYS BEEN AT HOME with martial arts. The city's legendary founder—Romulus—finished off his twin brother in a match that made him sovereign of the future metropolis that bears his name. The twins' father—Mars—god of war and Rome's protector, enjoyed sensational popularity throughout antiquity. The visible reminders of his bellicose empire lie scattered throughout the modern city. The Campus Martius or "Field of Mars" provided the stomping grounds where the Roman armies drilled and young patricians honed their martial skills. The Regia on the Forum Romanum stored the lances of Mars which when removed from their customary chamber to the mantra "Mars awaken!" signaled war, and the Colosseum welcomed gladiators who indulged their fascination through mortal combat in stylized ferocity to roaring spectators. At the base of this martial empire that spanned Northern African, most of Europe and the Middle East, lay the premise: All conflicts must end in victor and vanquished.

But must they? In 2008, a new martial art from Japan—Waraku—meaning "peace and goodness forever" established its

European center in Mars' own multicultural city. The Wako Dojo, a few steps from St. Peter's Basilica, opened with mirthful toasts of *saké* and the aspiration to spiral from Rome across Europe. Inspired by Japan's indigenous animistic religion—Shinto—this new martial art is, at least at this point in time, synonymous with its founder—Hiramasu Maeda—a native of Kyoto who has practiced martial arts since the age of 10. An Omoto-Shinto priest and former Olympic-class karate champion, Maeda embodies the apparent paradox of Waraku—a *martial* art based on the principle "not to hurt others and not to be hurt by others."

When asked about the apparent oxymoron—a *peaceful* martial art—Maeda insisted that although the Japanese term *budō* translates as "martial arts" in English, its real essence has been lost in translation. "The *budō* are not *martial* in origin," says the 56-year old Maeda (who has a physique resembling that of the statue of Mars in Palazzo Altemps), "but a type of religious practice that uses the physical body to get closer to the *kami*"—those numinous presences in the air, the mountains, the waters, and the human heart. The various *budō,* whether karate, kung fu, or tae kwon do, all teach a philosophy meant to be tested with the physical body; but when this becomes a corporal practice alone, divorced from any philosophy, one is left only with a sport. The problem as Maeda sees it is that the Japanese *budō* have long been associated with the samurai mentality of medieval Japan, or as techniques to train soldiers for modern warfare (the Japan Self Defense Forces are trained in judo and kendo), or as competitive sports from amateur tournaments to the Olympic Games.

This perception of *budō* as either aggressive killing arts or triumphing over a rival for prize or trophy has spread throughout the world but represents a deterioration of their original spirit that is allegedly to be found in ancient Shinto texts. Maeda's mission is largely to reorient the martial arts. "The *budoka* (martial artist) works for the divinity," said Maeda during a workshop held in Parma in July 2009. The practice aims at integrating the mental, physical, and emotional aspects of a person in exercises that couple sounds with body movements. Since Waraku teaches that the strongest power in the world is love and the weakest is hatred or the inability to forgive, Waraku bouts are not between "opponents" but rather "companions." The long wooden sword used in the martial art is likewise steeped in creative rather than destructive associations: To the untrained eye it is merely a long wooden stick, but to the initiated it is linked to the Shinto creation story when the heavenly parent of the Japanese people lowered a lance into the thick brine of sea. After turning it in a spiral movement, the islands of the archipelago emerged from the fluid chaos. Thus, the sword is dedicated to the divinity and venerated as if it were a statue of a saint.

The core of Maeda's teachings—a spiral—would have delighted both Fibonacci and Da Vinci who were likewise fascinated by the form. Fibonacci first determined that natural patterns of spiral growth exist throughout the universe. Consider the logarithmic spiral shape of the nautilus shell, the winding distribution of bracts on a pinecone, the clockwise and counterclockwise seed arrangements of sunflowers, or the spiral arms of whirling galaxies. The importance of the spiral for the martial art is the fact that it originates from a core and spirals outward in overlapping circles that gain energy with momentum. Maeda teaches reverence for the spiral both in its form and concept. Waraku practitioners learn to move with the rhythm of the universe says Maeda who teaches 75 different spiral movements. "By making a spiral movement toward your companion you repair his energy," says the master. Thus, Waraku is less a technique to protect oneself or to attack another than as a way to keep energy moving. The Waraku practitioner aspires to be a person who stirs an otherwise inert environment.

Now in existence for thirteen years, Waraku is actually an eclectic synthesis of all the techniques and philosophies that the charismatic Maeda has under his black belt. Though the list includes mastery of karate, short-term Zen training in the Nanzenji temple in Kyoto, and K-1 sport (karate, kenpo, kickboxing, and kung fu), Waraku's closest cousin is Aikido, a martial art that also drew from Shinto's theory of sound known as *kotodama*. In this system, certain sounds or vibrations are believed to have a latent power capable of influencing the mind, body, spirit, and the actual physical environment. The mother sounds (shared by both Japanese and Italian)—vowels *a, o, e, i*—form a spiral, and correspond to four points around the body where energy is believed to gather during certain maneuvers. These points are above, below, left, and right of a person and are named after the elements: heaven, earth, fire, and water. The center, envisioned as a fifth point or core that intersects all the points, corresponds to the vowel *u*. All the points, equidistant from the core, form a protective circle around the practitioner. The soul of a person also consists of four aspects—audacity, affinity, love, and wisdom—that continually interact with each other yet require discipline to be kept in balance. Since these different aspects of the soul correspond to prescribed sounds, the utterance of certain syllables or vowels can enhance a particular part of the soul.

Unlike the better-known Chinese system, in Waraku the human body has three energy points that run down the center. The first (*jôden*) lies where the third eye is perceived to be. The second (*chûden*) is the solar plexus area, and the third (*kaden*) is in the lower abdomen where Japanese tradition locates the *hara* or seat of life. These energy points govern the body's various movements in space and when properly aligned a person is well balanced with an energy that flows unobstructed.

Shinto's spiritual dimensions, as embodied in a practice such as Waraku, have long been eclipsed by the religion's popular association with kamikaze pilots in World War II and military aggression in Asia since the nineteenth century when Japan also dreamed of empire. However perverted for political ends, Shinto has always had a peaceful arm grounded in a profound reverence for nature. It is possible that Shinto may now be coming of age in a world fraught with environmental degradation and the secularism of much of Europe, and its growing rise in North America coupled with nostalgia for spirituality without the usual dogmatic baggage. In this sense, Shinto is particularly accessible. It makes no sharp distinction between the sacred and the secular since the particulars of daily life and the sacred whole are always mutually reflected in each other. Unadorned simplicity is Shinto's hallmark: The unpainted wood of its shrines, the loose gravel of its forest pathways, the minimalism expressed in its aleph-shaped gateways conspicuously lacking any fences (since they only serve to confine), and the absence of a textual tradition that might just bog a person down.

It is hardly a coincidence that Mars has welcomed this new martial art from the heartland of Japan into his ancient repertoire by housing it in the very center of his city. For Mars was never a simple god; he began his career as a deity of vegetation and fertility. He was a husband to more than one woman, a father to Romulus and Remus, and a lover to no one less than Venus. Yet his popularity as a war god all but effaced the pacifism of his early biography. In Waraku, both polarities of Mars are reconciled within a single practice. This can be experienced directly twice a year when Hiramasu Maeda comes from Kyoto to the Wako Dojo in Rome. During the rest of the year in Maeda gives teaches his growing band of peaceful warriors in Kyoto—both men and women, young and old—intent on cultivating the still center of their own whirling spirals.

Practical Information

Origin Arts Program
Iori Corporation
144-6 Sujiya-cho
Takatsuji-agaru,
Tominokoji-dori
Shimogyo-ku, Kyoto 600-8061
Tel: (075) 352-0211

Budo Waraku
Oomoto Headquarters
Ten'on-kyo, 1 Uchimaru
Aratsuka-cho
Kameoka-shi
Kyoto-fu, 621-8686
Tel: 771-22-5561

Escape to Reality
The *Mikkyo* of Issey Miyake's Fashion

I N BOTH HIS LIFE AND WORK contemporary fashion designer Issey Miyake has overturned some of the most dogged clichés about Japan. Gone is the *wabi-sabi* aesthetic of rustic simplicity that exalts dark intermediate colors, and in marches the splashy and flamboyant *basara* associated with the Namboku (1336-1392) period. Gone, too, is any sense of insularity, for Issey's cosmopolitan career has spanned Paris, London, New York, and Tokyo and blurred any neat national classification. The designer's insatiable appetite for technological innovation and uncanny intuition of the emptiness of forms (he makes garments of total reversibility, sometimes also equally fit to wear right-side up or upside-down) has introduced a sense of playfulness to his sartorial rendition of a central Buddhist tenet: Form is emptiness and emptiness is form. After all, for Issey a piece of clothing is unfinished or simply naked without a human body to celebrate it and spectators to enjoy it.

Despite his cosmopolitanism, the ghost of the kimono still haunts much of Issey's fashion. In interviews, the designer has claimed that the kimono has reached the end of its evolutionary course and achieved perfection. Therefore, rather than a slavish replication, Issey has deconstructed the form and applied the lessons learned from that cultural icon to contemporary and even futuristic motifs. One such lesson is the concept of "space" or *ma* that operates in other traditional Japanese arts such as calligraphy or karate. Within the framework of fashion, this means that Issey cultivates surplus space between the body and the garment. The ample wrap-around that constitutes the mainframe of the kimono has inspired the way he cuts cloth and ultimately manufactures sleeves. But given his profound awe for the French designer Madeleine Vionnet, responsible for introducing sewing on the bias through her Grecian-inspired gowns, merely reveals another avenue of Issey's quest for the perfect relationship between the body and fabric. Thus, the phantom kimono perceived in his designs tells only part of a complex story.

Though the kimono is unarguably an ethnic costume, within the context of Japan the dress possesses a universality because it favors no one sex or body type: young or old, fat and slim all easily wear the unfitted wrap. Perhaps most importantly, once cinched with the *obi*, the wearer is suddenly transformed into a quieter and more modest creature with steps that become mincing and movements more restrictive. Such is the way clothing shapes the wearer and inculcates cultural values. Issey would apply this rule in the service of his own values and liberate the wearer through a more expansive aesthetic based on *mikkyo* and its central aspiration—*sokushin jobutsu*—to become a buddha in this very body.

Steve Jobs observed a glimpse of this kind of sartorial power when he visited the Sony Corporation in the 1980s where Issey had designed one of the company's uniforms. The sleeves on the stylish rip-stop nylon jacket unzipped and morphed the piece into a vest. The way the whole flexible uniform served as a vehicle of bonding within Sony inspired Apple's founder to commission Issey to fashion a similar vest for Apple employees. Though ultimately the American work team proved too recalcitrant to wear any kind of explicit uniform, no matter the caliber of elegance,

Jobs asked Issey to make him some of the sweaters he admired. From this encounter was born the signature black mock-turtleneck associated with Apple's charismatic founder.

For Issey, ultimately the kimono stood as Japan's version of "A-POC," an acronym he coined for "A Piece of Cloth." According to Issey's theory, every civilization had begun its clothing career by making garments from a single piece of bark or cloth—the Indian sari, the Indonesian sarong, the Polynesian lava-lava, the Scottish kilt, or the Mongolian del. A-POC was as true for Greece as for Africa—whether round or rectangular, the concept of a single piece of cloth was an independent human invention everywhere. Prior to the advent of weaving, early humans still observed A-POC by wearing single animal pelts not only for protection but, in the words of maverick designer Friedensreich Hundertwasser, as a "second skin" that set them apart from other animals. The second skin increasingly served as a social passport: You are what you wear. All of fashion is an elaboration of this second skin. Whether our early ancestors with a pelt slung over the shoulder or, in more recent times, draped in a toga dyed royal purple from the mucus of a predatory sea snail, single pieces of cloth held in place with brooch or belt, knots or tucks mark our cultural and geographic diversity. For Issey, A-POC is simply the ground zero of fashion and the place to which he has returned repeatedly for inspiration.

In 1999, together with one of his disciples Dai Fujiwara, Issey introduced A-POC in Tokyo by presenting a knitted tube of elastic nylon, computerized cutting guides, and scissors that gave the potential wearers the option to customize a personal garment. The shape and length of sleeves and hemline, the curves or angles of the neckline all were choices for the consumer to make and cut right on the spot. Among other considerations, A-POC represented a response to the problem of sustainability in an industry plagued by rapid obsolescence. A-POC was meant to raise awareness that at the heart of the apparel industry lies simple waste—fabric scrap heaps destined to glut landfills. A-POC also contained an implicit critique of Western clothing as the *de facto* norm of modernity.

Japan's garment industry that developed rapidly in the 1960s as the country began rising like a phoenix after its defeat in Pacific War and occupation by the U.S. Allied Forces (1945-1952), encouraged women to abandon the kimono definitively as daily wear and adopt Western ready-to-wear clothing. The cut-and-sewn Western styles were fitted garments like those seen in Hollywood movies of the 1950s, whereas decades later A-POC intended to reassert the validity and integrity of the concept of a piece of cloth as an alternative modernity without falling into the trap of nostalgia through a simple reversion to the kimono. As Akiko Fukai has written, the idea first presented in 1974, and the one that launched Issey to fame was a piece-of-cloth, a two-dimensional dress—the basic concept of Japanese clothing.

Though A-POC represented a public experiment (the few people I met in Kyoto who had participated in such cutting "orgies" were enthusiastic), Issey is often associated exclusively with his most popular though more conservative perennial item—pleated slacks, dresses, and shirts in a line known as "Pleats Please," first introduced in 1993 and still a strong seller. Issey developed a method of his own to make pleats reminiscent of those made by the Spanish designer Mariano Fortuny whose still "classified" method of delicate pleating fascinated him. While most pleating methods create pleats in the fabric prior to sewing, Issey reversed the process by cutting and sewing lightweight polyester fabric into oversized garments pleated afterwards by feeding the item into a heat press protected by layers of *washi* or fibrous Japanese paper. Issey's pleats alternate in opposite directions like the folds on a paper fan. Perhaps at the heart of this love of pleats lies the phantasm of a fashion accessory—the fan—long cherished by Spaniards and Japanese alike.

Developed at the end of the 1980s, these pleated garments intended as daily wear represented Issey's indefatigable search to manifest a democratic ideal in clothing comparable to that wrought internationally by the mighty but humble dungarees. Breaking through cultural and class barriers, the simple denim trousers have traveled the globe and crossed all gender lines. With his pleats, Issey aimed at creating a garment that might also transform daily life on a grand scale. His pleats, seared into the fabric's memory by the heating process, do not disappear over time. The pleated clothing is crease-resistant, easy to wash, and quick to dry. But unlike the sturdy knock-around blue jeans, Issey's pleated line was perhaps too elegant and costly to ever be adopted for mass consumption. While popular, it seems to have a niche mostly among middle- and upper- middle class women. The pleated garments are elegant, travel well, and everyone knows the brand.

Perhaps the most attractive aspect of Issey's designs is that they seem to emerge from a celebration of life and conjure up the whole universe reminiscent of *mikkyo's* emphasis on the cosmic Buddha who permeates the universe. Amazingly light, not fitted but flowing so as to unfetter the body, the rich and vivid colors please the eye while zoomorphic, botanical, and futuristic motifs stimulate the imagination, these clothes seem to reintegrate the wearer into a vast cosmos. Kyoto philosopher Umehara Takeshi captured something of the excitement engendered by Issey's creations when he described the designer as an iconoclast who had broken with the *wabi-sabi* that has dominated Japanese aesthetics for hundreds of years and for reviving both the *basara* aesthetic and the vitality of Japan's prehistoric Jomon period.

Through his optimism and luminosity, Issey is continuously reinventing the present as a place we would like to live in. He communicates a deep appreciation for being alive by engaging the senses through the medium of cloth in a way that resonates with *mikkyo's* aspirations to get people back into their own skin—the first skin of the human body. *Mikkyo* also assigns a positive value to Buddhist ideas of impermanence, an area central to Issey's project. After all, there is no single way to wear his garments since they possess no stable identity. The person who wears the dress transforms it in a way that suggests the mutability of identity.

Precisely because of the high level of participation demanded of the wearer, Issey's designs require an ingenuity that raises the status of the person in his garments to that of an active co-creator. This also explains why some people claim that although they adore Issey's clothing they would never wear it themselves for lack of confidence.

The *Heart Sutra*, central to *mikkyo* and other schools of Mahayana Buddhism, may be summed up in the phrase: Form is emptiness and emptiness is form. Applied to clothing, this implies that the cloth by itself is not the garment, the shape is not the garment, and the function is not the garment. Rather, the garment is all of these things together with the human body that temporarily inhabits the garment along with those who appreciate it when encountered on a person in the real world.

References

Fukai Akiko. "Drapes and Pleats, or Japanese Fashion Design" (p. 97-109), In *Ptychoseis = Folds and Pleats: Drapery From Ancient Greek Dress to Twentieth Century Fashion*. Peloponnesian Folklore Foundation, Athens, 2004.

Isaacson, Walter. Steve Jobs. Simon & Schuster, New York, 2011, p. 361

Umehara Takeshi. "Issey Miyake: An Artist of "Basara" (p. 132-133), In *Issey Miyake Bodyworks*. Shogakukan, Tokyo, 1983.

Practical Information

Kobe Fashion Museum
9-1-2 Koyocho-naka
Higashinada, Kobe 658-0032
Tel: (078) 858-0050
www.fashionmuseum.or.jp/english/index.html

Issey Miyake Kobe
1 F NTT Nishinihon Shinkobe Bldg.
1 Maemachi, Chuo-ku, Kobe 650-0039
Tel: (078) 392-2223
www.isseymiyake.co.jp/en/news_test/stores/kobe/

ELTTOB TEP Issey Miyake
1F 4-11-28 Minamisemba
Chuo-ku, Osaka 542-0081
Tel: (06) 6251-8887
www.isseymiyake.co.jp/ELTTOB_TEP/en/semba/

Issey Miyake Boutique
Isetan Department Store
JR Kyoto Station Complex
Karasuma Shiokoji, Higashi Shiokoji-cho
Shimogyo-ku, Kyoto 600-8555
Tel: (075) 352-1111
www.wjr-isetan.co.jp/Kyoto/index.htm

CHAPTER 17

The Painting on the Walls
Hideki Kimura's Mural Art

A T A TIME WHEN THE "GALAPAGOSIZATION" of Japan is easily bandied about in conversation—by which is usually meant people's increasing withdrawal from civic life and the nation's disengagement from global society—evidence to the contrary comes as a sudden gust of fresh air into a hothouse. More surprising is the shape such evidence has taken in Kyoto, a city better known for the preservation of venerable traditions than contemporary innovation. Yet art in its most public medium—the mural—appears to be flourishing in the ancient capital. It turns up in unexpected places—enormous figures of elephants somersault across a parking lot fence, gargantuan white tigers fill the stairwell of a boutique hotel, a symphony of massive cobalt blue flora and fauna from pumpkins to praying mantises adorns the interior of a business complex, and a section of an underground mall teems with the legendary rush of carp swimming upward in the hope of becoming dragons in heaven.

Behind all these mammoth images of pulsating vitality is artist Hideki Kimura, 69, the son of a fisherman from Sakai. He's a prodigiously talented man who seems like an honorary ambassador

sent from the world of plants and animals to communicate with wayward humans. Kimura has always thought big—even when he was quite small and not yet in kindergarten. With a shard of slate in hand, Kimura drew murals on the ground at the request of his increasingly astonished neighbors, one of whom said he thought the young boy was the Hibari Misora of the painting world. Enka singer Misora also began her career as a child prodigy.

While those nursery-age commissions included figures from the realms of sumo and baseball, today Kimura's signature style consists exclusively of subjects from the plant and animal kingdoms drawn on a colossal scale. Some of these works are also in Hong Kong, South Korea, and the United States.

The influences of Kimura's murals can be teased out to some extent—the youth revolution of the 1960s and '70s, international currents in the world of modern art, and the resonances of

Japanese *ukiyo-e* aesthetics. In his student days at the Kyoto City University of Arts, Kimura came under the charismatic influence of Viennese Jewish émigré Felice Ueno-Rix, known to most simply as "Lizzi." Ueno-Rix came to Kyoto in the lat 1920s after marrying Isaburo Ueno, a Kyoto native who had worked as an architect in Berlin and Vienna. In Kyoto, the cosmopolitan duo became instrumental in the diffusion of European modernism in Japan.

Under Ueno-Rix's influence, Kimura developed a consciousness that would remain with him for life. In his work he has always aimed for international expression with a global scope that could at the same time brighten the civic life of his own city. While Ueno-Rix worked in a range of media, the artist's love of plants appeared abundantly in her textiles and wallpaper motifs lavish with fruit and floral imagery. To paint the murals she designed for the Actress restaurant in Tokyo's Nissay Theatre, Ueno-Rix selected Kimura and three other artists, as shown in the photo collection in Kimura's book *Muga Muchu* (Selfless Absorption).

While a seminal influence, Ueno-Rix was but one chord in Kimura's eclectic development. Other trendsetters of the time were inspirational—the multifaceted Sakai Naoki, who designed cameras for Olympus, the Nissan B-1 automobile that started a boom of cutely rounded cars, and sofas and phones for other major companies. After years in Paris, London and New York, fashion designer Issey Miyake established his headquarters in Tokyo. One of Kimura's design students—Makiko Minagawa—joined the Miyake Design Studio team from the start as a primary textile designer.

Though Kimura remained for a time as an instructor at his alma mater, the student activism and unrest left him increasingly dissatisfied in an academic setting. He turned from design instructor to the field of music and became a rock concert producer. Through rock music, Kimura imbibed a version of American culture that ultimately influenced his artistic credo: Direct, Simple, Easy, and Free. American pop artists also excited him. Blurring the line between popular and elite art, Andy Warhol,

Roy Lichtenstein and James Rosenquist employed advertising, comic books, and mundane objects in their work. Rosenquist had also worked as a billboardist, which influenced his later choice to create large-scale paintings. Much as he admired them, for Kimura, "American pop artists were speaking from the culture of New York. I wanted to realize Kyoto in pop art."

In Japan, pop artists draw heavily from anime and *ukiyo-e*. Takashi Murakami's superflat art movement makes a virtue of two-dimensionality as being quintessentially Japanese. Yoshitomo Nara's paintings of children, while looking partially like hostile versions of Margaret Keen waifs or Blythe dolls, are also reminiscent of anime characters. Part of the diffusion strategy of these artists (and pop artists generally) has been through commercial reproduction. Murakami has produced colored monograms for Luis Vuitton, and Nara has a limited wristwatch and clothing line that draws from his repertoire of motifs.

Kimura's organic imagery and vibrant color palette have lent themselves easily to attractive reproduction. Ki-Yan Stuzio in Kyoto's Gion district sells fabrics, canvas bags, shirts and ceramics with Kimura's dynamic designs. There is something both disarming and volcanic about Kimura's artistic expression. After 35 years of working only sporadically as a painter, Kimura finally surrendered himself at age 60 to painting as a full-time muralist. After all those years of incubation, he says, "I got the power to see."

His work sidesteps the cuteness aesthetic of many of his contemporaries. Kimura's colors often startle, such as the Venetian red of the panthers in a mural titled *Laughing Panthers* that stand starkly at a distance from each other. Since the luster of any animal—take fish, butterflies or fireflies—quickly fades once they are caught, the creatures in Kimura's vast menagerie are always depicted in their own habitats, even if highly stylized and fantastical. The delicately stepping pewter-colored storks painted on a pale grey cement wall at the Hirose Ladies Clinic in Fushimi, Kyoto Prefecture, exude a palpable vitality in spite of the subdued color scheme.

In eschewing theory in favor of "sensation" Kimura reveals his peculiar perspective and deep commitment to touch the essence of his subjects. Of art's many functions, one of them is certainly shamanic: to give people back to themselves and restore their spirits. These mammoth plants, but especially the animals, act as totems. In their presence we come back to an old place but in a completely new way.

Since murals defy the traditional exhibition format of collecting paintings under a single roof for viewing, the best way to see Kimura's work is to take a walk in central Kyoto. The Tendai temple of Shorenin Monzeki, famous for its National Treasure, a scroll of a blue Fudomyoo deity, also has three sets of *fusuma* or sliding walls on which Kimura has painted various kinds of lotuses. *Blue Fantasy* features giant blue lotuses, while *Praise Life* adds turtles and dragonflies, and *Paradise* is populated with lotuses of a brilliant red and yellow. A 15-minute walk from the temple is the Yonemura restaurant, where Kimura's giant burgundy shellfish *Lucky Lobster* flexes gracefully on the ceiling.

But perhaps the most impressive mural of all is that owned by the Kyoto City Zoo: *Gorillas' Daily Life*, which fills the interior of a building with an extended family of gorillas the color of lapis lazuli. Kimura's spirit seems to have ripened and opened to the whole of creation. Finding joy in even the smallest creatures, he magnifies them in his work with both passion and delicacy.

Practical Information

Shorenin Monzeki (Tendai sect)
69-1 Sanjobo-cho Awataguchi
Higashiyama-ku, Kyoto 605-0035
Tel: (075) 561-2345
www.shorenin.com

Kyoto City Zoo
Okazaki Hoshojicho
Sakyo-ku, Kyoto 606-8333
Tel: (075) 771-0210
www5.city.kyoto.jp/zoo

Yonemura Restaurant (Reservations required)
481-1 Kiyoicho, Yasaka Toriimae-sagaru
Higashiyama-ku, Kyoto 605-0821
Tel: (075) 533-6699
www.r-yonemura.jp

Ki-Yan Stuzio
292-2 Gionmachi Kitagawa
Higashiyama-ku, Kyoto 605-0073
Tel: (075) 525-0625
www.ki-yan-stuzio.com

PART V

YOUTH CULTURE

A Dream of One's Own
Lolita in Rococo, Japan

ASHION CAN BE A FORM OF STATUS DISPLAY, a personal identity laboratory, an act of outright insurgency, or some combination of these. In a country where uniforms are required from kindergarten through high school, after-school hours may turn into explosive celebrations of individual taste and style, and provide the impetus for a vibrant culture of street fashion. When the first Lolitas began to appear in some critical mass in the youth meccas of Harajuku in Tokyo and Amerika-mura in Osaka, the dress was shocking not because of any overly erotic display but rather for the outlandish modesty and unabashed exhibition of what appeared to be an anachronistic femininity. Where had it come from?

Although this was the 1980s when mainstream Japanese culture was inundated with all things *kawaii* or "cute" (and Hello Kitty had achieved unofficial national mascot status), there was still something unsettling about contemporary young Japanese women who chose to dress in the modest yet frilly clothing of Victorian-era girls. The lacy flat-bodiced dresses they wore with full skirts and voluminous underskirts fell just below the knees where they met with high stockings or frilly garters. Over the dress a white or pastel apron completed the ensemble. In addition, the nubile girls curled their hair in ringlets tied with satiny ribbons, fastened with an elaborate headband, or hidden shyly under a full peek-a-boo bonnet. Their shoes displayed big bows, and they carried a small purse, a stuffed animal or a doll look-alike in one hand and perhaps a parasol in the other. In fact, highly codified, the outfit might easily be read as another kind of uniform. But why had they invented it?

This hyper-femininity represented the original Sweet Lolita style, the foundational template, inspired in part by *Alice in Wonderland*, Victorian porcelain dolls, and Japanese notions of the French Rococo. Although a strong spirit of DIY prevailed and encouraged those involved in the subculture to create their own style and imaginative self, the Lolita look expanded in popularity with the emergence of brands aimed at girls from their teens to mid-twenties. The first, Baby, The Stars Shine Bright appeared in 1988, and Manifesteange Metamorphose Temps de Fille in 1993. By then Lolita existed as an entrenched fashion subculture, and the elaborate garments required a significant investment in both time and money. An entire outfit, especially if accessorized with Vivienne Westwood rocking-horse ballerina shoes, could easily cost $1,000. As for time, Lolita could only be indulged in after-school hours and on weekends when these young girls could be seen streaming into areas around Shinsaibashi in Osaka or in the makeshift promenades—the coned-off streets of Tokyo's Omotesando and Takeshita.

Were the Lolita look only skin-deep—a mere fashion fad—it would not have survived long in Japan nor ever managed to reach and grip a global audience in Asia and the Western countries where Lolita subcultures now thrive. Yet from an apparent fashion statement, Lolita evolved into a lifestyle with its own ethos, speech patterns, mannerisms, and behaviors. Even the dress itself diversified rapidly to accommodate variations as the Lolita community grew and spawned various subgenres: Gothic Lolita, Punk

Lolita, Wa Lolita, Princess Lolita, or Sailor Lolita. Some of these were clearly hybrids. For instance, the so-called Country Lolita combined elements of the Sweet Lolita with those of the Classic Lolita but could be distinguished from both by the straw baskets to be carried instead of purses and the gingham-patterned dress. The Wa Lolita (Japanese Lolita) incorporated a modified kimono bodice with the usual bell-shaped skirt but then added high platform sandals (*okobo*) normally worn by geisha. Lolita combinations were potentially limitless.

In 2001, *The Gothic & Lolita Bible* debuted as a quarterly publication devoted to the Lolita lifestyle though with an overwhelming focus on the genre of the Sweet Lolita. Intended as the definitive source of information on Lolita fashion, it helped consolidate the community and standardize the style. The publisher touted not only the novelty of its contents but the form itself: Neither quite a book nor a magazine, it was given the hybrid name of a "mook" (*mukku*). The mook contained a section on proper speech etiquette dubbed the "Gentleman and Lady's Gothic & Lolita Manner Encyclopedia" that introduced an idealized women's language resurrected from prewar models. Here Lolitas could learn to use polite but archaic verb conjugations ending in—seu, elaborate honorifics, and feminine sentence-endings. The mook also featured photos of correct posture, facial expressions, ladylike ways to walk as well as offering fashion advice, sewing patterns in the spirit of DIY, and interviews with Lolita trendsetters.

Ranking among the top was novelist Takemoto Novala (b. 1968) featured also in the English version of *The Gothic & Lolita Bible* launched in the U.S. in 2008. From the tea-producing region of Uji just outside of Kyoto, Takemoto was already known for his critically acclaimed collection of essays, *Soleilnuit: For Becoming a Proper Young Lady*, before his 2002 novel *Kamikaze Girls* became a an international hit and was followed by the movie two years later that earned him a cult following and a global fan base. The film and novel transformed Takemoto into a champion of the Lolita lifestyle and eventually into a collaborator with Baby,

The Stars Shine Bright on a label of his own: Novala Takemoto POUR LOLITA.

Takemoto's *Kamikaze Girls*, a coming of age story, revolves around an intense friendship between two high school girls who belong to different subcultures. Ichigo is a so-called Yanki, a member of the all-girl biker gang Ponytails, while Momoko is a Sweet Lolita devoted to a French Rococo lifestyle albeit in contemporary Japan. Both girls live in the small town of Shimotsuma in Ibaraki Prefecture some two hours by train from Tokyo though it feels to them worlds away. They are strong-willed loners who somehow manage to nourish their own set of values and in so doing have a sense of belonging to an elect minority of individualists within a larger culture whose ideology and expectations they wholeheartedly resist.

In an interview with the *Asahi Shimbun* in 2004, Takemoto said: "Lolita is a form of aestheticism. I think Lolita is a condition in which two conflicting elements co-exist without contradiction, for example, something grotesque as well as cute...A Lolita loves *Alice in Wonderland* because the chaotic situation in Wonderland is very Lolita-like." As early as the first chapter in *Kamikaze Girls*, the Lolita protagonist—Momoko—articulates a few features of this complicated aesthetic:

- Only in Rococo—elegant yet in bad taste, extravagant yet defiant and lawless—can I discover the meaning of life.
- For me, Lolita goes far beyond fashion and serves as my unwavering, absolute personal policy.
- If I didn't dress in this totally conspicuous and bizarre way, I'd make friends and be popular with boys.

The ornate dress then is clearly not worn to be sweet and demure, or become the object of someone else's desire, but instead is an act of defiance. The hyper-feminine clothing creates a boundary around those who wear it. Empowered by an aesthetic that allows an imaginary flight from Japan, Lolitas seek sanctuary in a foreign time and place largely of their own invention. In effect, they create a caricature of France or England rather than simple mimicry. Nevertheless, the protagonist defends the Rococo as an era generally treated as a blot on history and thus carefully relegated to oblivion presumably by stodgy historians. Following in the wake of the solemn masculinity of the Baroque described as "serious," "boring," and "oppressive," the Rococo is by contrast "fanciful," "ornate," and "feminine." It is also a time when even men were supposedly feminized.

Given the doll-like persona, the Lolita style is frequently misread within and outside Japan as girls attempting to be seductive by playing the role of innocents. The term *rorii-kon* (Lolita Complex) in Japanese refers to men obsessed with young girls and has even produced a genre of *manga* that caters to the fantasies of such men. (Yes, these are the same ones who purchase recycled schoolgirls' uniforms and underpants.) Since the name presumably derives from Vladimir Nabokov's novel *Lolita*, an unfortunate overlap exists for actual Lolitas who have created an alternative social world where they can display modesty and elegance. This is also a dream space where they venture to express an authentic self that they refer to as a "princess."

The darker version of Lolita finds expression in the genre called Gothic Lolita that gained momentum in the late 1990s. These Lolita dress in elegant black frilly frocks and project a more experienced, or even jaded persona. The Gothic got its boost from the visual-kei rock band Malice Mizer. The group's crossdressing guitarist Mana adopted the dress and popularized the look. He then produced his own clothing brand and store: Moimême-Moitié. Whether Gothic or Sweet, both poles of Lolita actively cultivate the lifestyle of a "princess." A princess is a person free to pursue her own interests and hobbies. She lives a charming life with her authentic self.

To appreciate the alternative world that Lolitas have fashioned requires a view of Japanese society during the transformative decades of the 1980s and 1990s. According to psychologist Iwao

Sumiko, author of *The Japanese Woman: Traditional Image and Changing Reality*, women in the mid-1980s began to speak of a "consciousness gap" between themselves and their partners. No longer was the corporate samurai an object of unquestioning desire but reassessed as a pitiful workaholic. By 1997, the birthrate in Japan had hit an all-time low (1.39) and the marriage age risen not only to the highest ever for Japan (29 for men and 27 for women) but the highest of any industrial country. Women turned increasingly to the international sphere in search of an alternative niche to the traditional ready-made female life course awaiting them. In this context, the foreign had become an important material and symbolic resource to resist the gendered expectations. Women's pursuit of foreign language study, study abroad, overseas employment, or work at an international company was a response to women's changed expectations.

Lolitas also turned to the foreign but as a symbolic resource. They were hardly suffering from nostalgia and a wish to return to simpler Victorian times or to a more ornate Rococo era. They were also not in pursuit of mere cuteness. Often ridiculed for their excess, Lolitas were dealing with the problem of women's limited options on an imaginary level through the symbolic language of fashion. The outlandish costume challenged prosaic futures as office ladies (OLs) who prepare tea and make endless photocopies. Lolitas criticized the norm by standing outside it in bold visual contrast. They may have been merely stalling for time, but in that interim Lolitas created a space in which to dream of a possible self within an imaginable Japan.

Practical Information

Kyoto
Baby, The Stars Shine Bright (Sweet Lolita)/h. Naoto (Punk Lolita)
OPA, 7th Floor, Shijo-agaru
Kawaramachi-dori, Nakagyo-ku, Kyoto
Tel: (075) 255-8111
www.babyssb.co.jp
www.hnaoto.com

Osaka (Amerika-mura)
Metamorphose temps de fille (EGL or Elegant Gothic Lolita)
13-18-4 Minamisemba
Chuo-ku, Osaka 542-0081
Tel: (06) 4704-6400
www.metamorphose.gr.jp

Marble (Gothic Lolita)
Nyuu-Amerikan Plaza, 3F-B
1-16-12 Nishi-Shinsaibashi
Chuo-ku, Osaka 542-0086
Tel: (06) 6252-0607
http://marble.girly.jp

CHAPTER 19

Manga Sanctuaries

A S A KID I GREW UP WATCHING the original black-and-white *Astro Boy* on TV and its later color version, never suspecting then that he was anything but a homegrown American robot with outstanding cowlicks. Years later in a conversation with an editor in Tokyo my same age we laughed with surprise and delight to discover that we had watched identical episodes in the same year—1963—he in Tokyo and I on the outskirts of Washington D.C. This was America's first taste of Japanese *anime* (Japanese animation film), and like the bulk of this genre it was created on the basis of a hit *manga* (the name for Japanese comics), in this case *Astro Boy or Tetsuwan Atom* meaning "Iron-Arm Atom" in Japanese, a serial that began in 1952 and ran for 17 years in *Shonen* magazine.

Astro Boy's creator—Tezuka Osamu (1928-1989), a great pioneer if not the sole "father" of Japanese *manga*—shaped the medium as we know it today by assimilating multiple aesthetic streams. He got the idea for the huge starry eyes of his characters partly from the lime-lit faces of the stars in the all-female musical troupe—the Takarazuka Revue Company—based in his hometown and whose theater he frequented with his mother as a boy and remained an avid fan throughout his life. Bambi, which he watched over 80 times, and Betty Boop were other strong early influences. Besides frequenting movie houses, Tezuka's father held home movie nights, and set up the family projector to show French, German, American, and Japanese flicks. All of these would infuse Tezuka's *manga* style with what were then surprisingly novel cinematic techniques. He employed pans, zooms, and angled perspectives that set the flat page in motion.

Comic strips translated from American newspapers appeared frequently in their Japanese counterparts as early as the 1920s and brought George McManus's *Bringing Up Father*, Bud Fisher's *Mutt and Jeff*, and Pat Sullivan's *Felix the Cat* into Japanese homes. Such crosscurrents between Japan and Western nations, especially the U.S., have been incessant for so many decades that distinguishing among them in the manner of "who got what from whom" easily becomes an entangling exercise in futility (1).

Through the largely democratic medium of *manga*, Tezuka was able to cross not only the horizontal divide of national boundaries but also the rather taboo vertical one of class and educational opportunity within his own country. My first glimpse of Tezuka's Promethean role occurred during a conversation with a middle-aged woman in eastern Osaka who had joined a charismatic Buddhist organization there. She confided to me rather bashfully that Tezuka Osamu's *manga Buddha* had led her to seek deeper spiritual involvement culminating in her eventual membership in the present religious community. But in fact, everything she knew about Buddhism had come initially from that 2,886-page epic *manga* serialized from 1972 to 1983, and ultimately collected into a 12-volume set. In its book format alone *Buddha* has sold over 9 million copies in Japan.

East Asian scholar Mark Wheeler MacWilliams, noting the gap between Buddhist scriptures and the common person, wrote that: "difficulties of access, readability, and length put them out of reach of most people." (2) However, Tezuka managed to make

the Buddha's story come alive as a spiritual tale for a modern Japanese mass audience jaded by the long association of Buddhism with the lucrative funeral industry. This *manga* transgressed the class boundary between "high" and "low" traditions, a feat Tezuka achieved (readers beware) by employing a storyteller's license to embroider, expand, and invent when it might enhance the entertainment value of this historical saga of the life of Siddhartha Gautama, the Buddha.

Prior to the establishment of the modern *manga* industry in which Tezuka's role remained pivotal, thousands of outdoor performers—*kami-shibai*—or traveling storytellers worked from miniature mobile theater boxes through which they slid pictures cards in one side and out the other. Legendary horror *manga* artist—Shigeru Mizuki—in his early career first worked drawing the picture cards for publishers who supplied these traveling storytellers at a time when outdoor theater was one of the only forms of entertainment a destitute population could afford. According to Paul Gavett in *Manga: Sixty Yeas of Japanese Comics*, approximately 10,000 traveling storytellers performed daily for an audience of nearly 5 million people. Though the heyday of *kami-shibai* was in the early post war period, these paper-card theaters could still be seen in the streets as late as 1953.

As *manga* developed further, artists who had worked as producers of cards for the *kami-shibai* such as Mizuki gravitated into another growing market to make stories for the new rental-library *manga* publishers. Mostly clustered in Osaka, these specialist companies produced hardbound books and magazines of limited runs to distribute to book-rental shops called *kashihonya* that served a function for *manga* much like Netflix or Tsutaya in the realm of DVDs today. According to Sharon Kinsella in *Adult Manga*, from the mid- to late-1950s, around 30,000 of these book-rental outlets could be found at train stations and street kiosks from which books could be rented for two days at a meager fee of 10-yen apiece. Like the *kami-shibai*, these rental *manga* provided one of the only affordable entertainment options at the time.

Osaka was also the hub of *akabon* or "red book" publishing. Local publishers commissioned these pocketsize *manga* printed on cheap paper with ample red ink, and had them sold unconventionally by street vendors or in candy stores. After the publication of Tezuka's *New Treasure Island* in *akabon* format, sales went off the charts causing a craze for *akabon manga* in the Kansai area. As their popularity grew so did the length of the stories along with the price. This together with the arrival of TV broadcasting in 1953 were largely responsible for the demise of both the *kashihonya* and the *akabon*. Once television started to become a fixture in Japanese homes from 1960 onwards, these publications could hardly compete.

Two Tokyo publishing giants—Kodansha and Shogakukan—had the insight to realize that part of the success of TV and radio derived from its format of airing weekly episodes. Up until this point most *manga* had been published in monthly installments. The two publishers decided to quicken the pace of *manga* and shift to the same weekly format as the rising star of TV. Both began their new weeklies in 1959 and as readers came to prefer the swifter pace of these weeklies the artists who produced them groaned under the workload. The greater frequency required that prominent artists now manage studios with their own assistants. Tezuka left Kansai and moved to Tokyo where he employed some thirty *manga* assistants. Thus, from Kansai the center of gravity of *manga* shifted definitively to Tokyo. But rather than being competitors TV and *manga* were mutually supportive since the serialized *manga* stories were inevitably adapted for TV animation which in turn served to advertise the *manga* and increase both its sales and longevity.

Manga's phenomenal range of themes and genres has fostered a dizzying variety of publications and niche markets. The four general categories are: boys' *manga* (shonen *manga*), girls' *manga* (shojo *manga*), adult *manga* (seinen), and adult women's *manga* (rediisu *manga*). The subcultural status of *manga* in its high-growth stage, plus the existence of such a genre as girls' *manga*, both facilitated women's breaking into the *manga* world in the early 1970s as writers without the resistance they would inevitably have faced in more mainstream media. Up until this point, men had written girls' *manga* for such popular monthlies as *Nakayoshi* (Good Friends) or *Shojo Club* (Girls' Club). Tezuka's first *manga* aimed at a female audience—*Princess Knight*—was serialized by both of these magazines at different times. It told the story of a girl with two souls—one, that of a battling knight, and the other a gentle princess. By means of this story, Tezuka paid homage to the Takarazuka theater he had admired since his boyhood where princes were played by dashing young female actresses.

The great appeal of the girls' *manga* genre resided in its emphasis on ordinary Japanese girls as heroines. Women *manga* artists eventually came to dominate the genre. Those from the immediate postwar period—Moto Hagio, Riyoko Ikeda, Yumiko Oshima, Keiko Takemiya, and Riyoko Yamagishi—had all cut their teeth on Tezuka's *manga* although they carried the medium into unchartered territory. They were expert at creating mood and emotion through novel collage-style graphics and special emoticon doodles.

In an era before social networks such as MIXI or Facebook existed, these women can be considered proto-bloggers. They often wrote notes in margins of their *manga* to chat about themselves or give their opinions and tastes. They also encouraged their young readers to send them cards with their questions or comments. This interactivity created a greater intimacy between manga artist and reader that fostered long-lasting bonds.

One of the all-time most popular girls' *manga*—Riyoko Ikeda's *The Rose of Versailles*—was published in 1972. A historical romance of 1,700 pages, it introduces two women during the French Revolution—Queen Marie-Antoinette married as a child to a crown prince though she loves a Swedish count, and Oscar, a girl raised as a nobleman because her father wanted a son instead. Ikeda's *manga* sold over 12 million copies in Japan, was adapted into a TV series, a live action film shot in Versailles, and a Takarazuka musical. *The Rose of Versailles* also became a centerpiece within Lolita culture.

In the 1990s *manga* faced a new challenge with the rapid expansion of computer games, personal computers, and the Internet. The profit rates were dropping and the industry appeared to be in decline. The 2000s would add smart phones to this list of entertainment devices that might usurp the place of *manga* as prime companion on the long subway commutes faced by millions of people daily. With the prolonged recession, 24-hour *manga* cafes (*manga* kissaten), began to pop up across the country. They represent a hybrid institution. Library, Internet café, and capsule hotel rolled into one, they exist on the fringes of kissaten culture. Their immediate purpose is clearly a library for *manga* aficionados with rows of towering shelves containing millions of paperback *manga*. For an hourly fee customers receive a cheap drink and can sit and read in an environment with vending machines, Internet stations, and even a few business booths decked out with executive chairs and slippers. Some *manga* cafes even have showers for an extra fee, rental towels, and lucky for those who miss the last train home, special sleeping booths for under $15 a night.

The bathrooms generally have high-tech washlet toilets. *Manga* cafes have proliferated in the recession years. While some of these cafes require member cards, the Popeye chain with outlets in all major cities is open to anyone.

Manga has progressively migrated from its original subcultural status from scruffy to cool and now into official governmental channels of popular culture diplomacy and on into academia. In 2000, Kyoto Seika University created the first Department of *Manga* and *Manga* Art in Japan. In partnership with the city of Kyoto in 2006, the university created The *Manga* Museum, a research facility and venue for the collection, preservation, and exhibition of *manga* and animation. Covering three floors, the museum's library contains over 50,000 publications, including a section of Japanese *manga* translations in 13 languages, and a section on international *manga* from Asian and European countries. The second floor has permanent display on the history of *manga* and anime with signboards in both English and Japanese. The university also launched its Ph.D. program in *manga* studies in 2012, two years after having initiated its M.A. Oriented towards teaching the feature-length story lines and not "funnies," graduates are expected to become *manga* artists, producers or publishers of manga, or researchers in the field of *manga*.

If that is not enough to highlight the utter mainstreaming and promotion of *manga* as a homegrown cultural product with global clout, in 2003 the fictional character Astro Boy was granted legal resident status in the city of Niiza in Saitama prefecture outside of Tokyo. The official document lists Professor Ochanomizu (his adopted father in the *manga* story) as the head of household, and Tezuka Productions as their legal residence. Art can't get much closer to life than this.

Practical Information

The Osamu Tezuka *Manga* Museum
7-65 Mukogawa-cho
Takarazuka-shi, Hyogo 665-0844
Tel: (0797) 81-2970
www.city.takarazuka.hyogo.jp/tezuka

Mizuki Shigeru Museum
5 Honcho
Sakaiminato, Tottori 684-0025
Tel: (0859) 42-2171
http://mizuki.sakaiminato.net

The Kyoto International *Manga* Museum
452 Kinbuki-cho, Karasuma Oike
Nagagyo-ku, Kyoto 604-0846
Tel: (075) 254-7414
www.kyotomm.jp/english

Media Café Popeye
42-6 (B1) Ebisu-cho
Kawaramachi Sanjo-agaru
Nakagyo-ku, Kyoto 604-8005
Tel: (075) 253-5300
www.mediacafe.jp/

Graduate School of *Manga*
Kyoto Seika University
International Office
137 Kinocho, Iwakura
Sakyo-ku, Kyoto 606-8588
Tel: (075) 702-5199
www.kyoto-seika.ac.jp/eng/edu/graduate/*manga*/

Notes

1 Roland Kelts. *Japanamerica: How Japanese Pop Culture Has Invaded the U.S.* Palgrave MacMillan, NY, 2007.

2 MacWilliams, Mark W. "Japanese Comic Books and Religion: Osamu Tezuka's Story of the Buddha," In *Japan Pop! Inside the World of Japanese Popular Culture*, ed. Timothy J. Craig, 109-137. M.E. Sharpe, Armonk, NY, 2000.

References

Paul Gravett. *Manga: Sixty Years of Japanese Comics.* HarperCollins. NY, 2004.

Sharon Kinsella. *Adult Manga: Culture & Power in Contemporary Japanese Society.*
Routledge Curzon. London/NY, 2000.
Helen McCarthy. *The Art of Osamu Tezuka: God of Manga.* Abrams ComicArts, NY, 2009.

CHAPTER 20

The Many Dimensions
of Anime

T HE FLIP SIDE TO THE LUMINOUS and lyrical anime of Miyazaki Hayao is the darker and quirkier vision of Satoshi Kon. Part funhouse, part psychological thriller, and part social commentary, Kon's anime explores the edginess of life in wealthy postindustrial Japan. It's a world where the tarpaulin and cardboard villages of the homeless teeter in the shadowy margins of the capital's luxury skyscrapers (*Tokyo Godfathers*), and where youth violence takes offbeat forms—a boy on rollerblades who bludgeons his victims with a baseball bat, and internet suicide clubs that bring strangers together in order to die (*Paranoia Agent*). Kon's work acts also as a cultural and historical echo chamber. The film about a legendary movie-star-turned-recluse takes us through the rise of modern Japan and its colonial legacy while illuminating the inner life of a famous actress (inspired partly by the real-life star Setsuko Hara of *Tokyo Story* fame) who squanders away her emotional life in pursuit of a stranger she meets as a teenager only to find out he has been dead throughout most of her quest (*Millennium Actress*). It's a world that manufactures teenage pop-idols with ephemeral careers whose own malignant alter-egos lash back and destroy them (*Perfect Blue*). All of these films blur what is real and unreal in ways that confound, challenge, and entertain as they break down a linear sense of time through the intrusion of memory that jumbles the present with the past, and the conscious with the subconscious into a grand montage.

Kon died in 2010 at the much too early at age of 46, leaving as his crowning achievement a heroine named Paprika whose survival after plumbing the depths as a dream detective stands as a paean to the potential for mending psychological fractures and re-establishing wholeness. The film's spicy heroine is not even a "real" character but rather the alter-ego of the film's psychiatrist, a devoted dream therapist (*Paprika*). Through casting the fantastical counterpart as the victorious character in a byzantine sci-fi adventure, Kon is suggesting that fantasy is a necessity and may be the only thing in the long run that keeps a person sane. He said as much in an interview with author Andrew Osmond in *Satoshi Kon The Illusionist*: "In order to live in reality, one must have room for fantasy, whether in the form of a myth, a folktale, a piece of music, a novel, or a film. Even religion can be considered as a form of fantasy. To need these hopes and dreams is human." (1)

Kon's position casts light on the abundance of Japanese urban spaces dedicated to imaginary worlds. Theater is everywhere. Quite apart from the castle-kitsch of love hotels that pepper the urban landscapes of Japan, themed restaurants and cafes are better nested in the quotidian. Take the Ninja Kyoto, for example, where waiters wearing ninja garb lead diners down a labyrinth and into private hideaways to dine. Or Tokyo's Alcatraz E.R., a medical prison-themed restaurant in which waitresses dress as nurses and serve their "patients" whose tables are placed in individual prison cells. Like something that escaped from the nearby Tokyo Disneyland, the family restaurant Alice in Wonderland, has waitresses in girly Victorian frocks and aprons. There are also maid cafes where the servers, attired as French au pairs, welcome their "masters" and "mistresses" *home* as they enter the establishment. Sister cafes have mock-cathedral interiors and waitresses in habit, while the waiters in butler cafes speak and dress with the formality of a bygone era. There are even little sister cafes where servers in school uniform ask advice of their customers and pretend, well, to be the your little sister.

With such a robust capacity to suspend disbelief either for the sheer fun of it or as Kon suggests—fantasy is a necessity—I was hardly surprised to hear of the petition filed by Takashita Taichi on Shomei TV's website on 22 October 2008. An obsessive anime fan or *otaku*, Takashita petitioned the Japanese government to legally recognize 2D marriage. Within a week 1,000 people expressed their support and within two months 3,000 more spoke up according to Ian Condry's report in *Recreating Japanese Men*. Takashita's proposal was not an abstract philosophical one either; he claimed to be smitten by Mikuru Asahina, a cute, petite, and large-bosomed, time-traveling girl from the future. He had met her on the anime *The Melancholy of Suzumiya Haruhi* that had aired two years previous to his petition though the story itself, based on the light novel or *ranobe* (a genre between manga and literature) series by Tanigawa Negaru, had been in circulation since 2005. Though Takashita's petition raised both eyebrows and passionate discussions both online and off, in the academy and in the coffeehouse, the Japanese marriage law has remained unchanged.

But Takashita hardly stood alone in his pursuit and passion for the two-dimensional. In Toru Honda's 2005 book *Radiowave Man (Denpa Otoko)*, the pseudonomous author was advocating a 2D lifestyle with rich anti-bourgeois overtones. The "love revolution" (*rei no kakumei*) of which he wrote was intended to challenge the commonplace: "love = 3D world". In fact, within Honda's technological scheme of civilization, those who do not opt for 2D are basically Luddites. Just as VCR necessarily gave way to the DVD, or analog to digital, the analog world of love for real women must ultimately give way to the digital world of characters. If love and romance have become mere commodities supported by a massive entertainment industry in the late 20th century, 2D love is one form of resistance to its perpetuation into the 21st.

Manifestations of 2D love are visible elsewhere and form an integral part of current otaku subculture. *Dakimakura* or "hug-pillows" are another desired 2D love object. These are costly, body-sized pillowcases with life-sized images of pop-idols or anime girls on them. In a report by Lisa Katayama for the *New York Times* (2), the 37-year-old "Nisan" (meaning older brother) carried such a pillowcase everywhere and referred to it or rather the 2D depiction of the character Nemu on the stuffed pillowcase as his girlfriend. Bikini-clad with ribboned hair, Nemu derived from the X-rated PC videogame Da Capo where she was the little sister of the main character. These pillowcase relations are not to be confused with situations dramatized in the films such as *Lars and The Real Girl* (2007) where a man is convinced (at least temporarily) that his doll-companion is a real woman. The owner of the pillowcase-girlfriend is entirely conscious of the fact that Nemu is not "real" but nevertheless claims the right to love her and consider her his girlfriend. The two have taken trips together, eat out at restaurants, and Nemu is carried upright as a standing person.

A subculture of men and women who have real relationships with imaginary characters is part of contemporary otaku subculture in Japan that revolves around obsessive dedication to *anime, manga* and video games. The word "otaku" itself means "your house" or "your family" in Japanese and is basically a formal and impersonal form of the pronoun "you." It carries the implication that relations between people who refer to each other as such are meant to be exchanges of information about mutual hobbies and interests and not about each other's personal lives.

According to public intellectual, Toshio Okada, one of the founders of animation studio Gainax, "An otaku is someone who is smarter than average people but chooses to divert their mental ability to childish hobbies. It's about *not* quitting the things that enthralled you as a kid. It isn't childish. An otaku is not a loser or someone who can only understand childish things. They understand high culture such as fine art but nonetheless insist that anime and manga are better" (3). For Okada, who defines himself as an otaku, the true otaku has all but disappeared from Japan since there is no longer a shared culture but many isolated individuals pursuing personal interests.

Increasingly, both the characters of anime and the aesthetics derived from them have spilled out beyond films, printed pages, and game-stations. Anime may function more as a place of encounter or "venue" that allows the initial contact with a character whose relationship may then continue in other formats. A bond with a character intensifies as the experiences diversifies—reading a *manga* or light novel, reencountering the same character within interactive videogames, a TV series, a feature-length anime, and into character goods such as *gochapan* or small detailed figurines sold in capsules from huge gumball machines. Social networks such as Mixi (Japan's largest social networking site) and popular video-sharing websites such as Nico Nico Douga and YouTube have created online venues where otaku can meet, stream video, and post comments, all of which heighten the experience and intensify involvement with 2D characters.

This is certainly the way in which the Vocaloid Hatsune Miku was launched into stardom and now enjoys over 830,000 fans on her Facebook page. A Japanese pop-idol, Hatsune Miku is also an imaginary character with neither *manga* nor *anime* to her credit. Yamaha Corporation developed the Vocaloid, a voice synthesizer software, that allowed users to produce singing from their computers by simply typing in lyrics and choosing the melody. A third-party developer, Crypton Future Media, then created the virtual idol to embody the synthesized voice to include with the software package. Hatsune Miku epitomizes the anime aesthetic with her saucer-eyes, cascade of ankle-length turquoise pigtails, trim figure, and big boobs. Released in 2007, Crypton markets the software as a "girl in a box."

Of all the Vocaloid produced to date, Hatsune is by far the most popular and her voice synonymous with the technology.

Her popularity also grew exponentially as users of the software posted their own original songs using her voice on Nico Nico Douga. This sharing fueled a music revolution that demanded something even bigger—a "live" performance. Hatsune has since performed in concert as a 3D hologram projection to full stadiums in Japan. In 2009, she went on tour to the U.S. and Singapore as the world's first virtual pop-idol.

Love of anime characters does not necessarily remain 2D forever. Bome, an early collaborator with artist Murakami Takashi (pioneer of a style known as "Superflat"), is one of the most renowned figure sculptors in Japan. He works in a studio at the Kaiyodo Company in Osaka known widely for its garage kits, monsters, and anime figurines. The unassuming Bome could easily be a solo artist but chooses artisan over artiste and specializes in rendering into 3D the 2D *bishojo* or "beautiful girls" figures found in manga and anime. His figures have been displayed in art spaces worldwide in exhibitions with Takashi Murakami. The Kaiyodo Figure Museum near Lake Biwa in Shiga has one of the largest repositories of model figures anywhere with approximately 200 dioramas and thousands of figures. The major sculptors of various genres have their own exhibition space here: Yamaguchi Katsuhisa for *mecha* (giant robots) and anime, Kagawa Masahiko for classic anime, and, of course, Bome with his beautiful anime girls.

Given the massive popularity of anime and other forms of Japanese pop culture, in 2006, Ministry of Foreign Affairs (MOFA) launched its Cool Japan initiative urging the Japanese business community to work with diplomats to promote popular culture –anime, manga, J-pop, and fashion. Embassies, consulates, and Japan External Trade Organization (JETRO) offices outside Japan began to promote "soft power" through manga contests, J-pop concerts and anime screenings. In 2008 MOFA named Fujiko Fujio's anime character Doraemon (a cultural icon since 1969) as anime Ambassador of Japan. This robot-cat from the 22nd century is loved both for the traditional values he inculcates as for the thousands of future gadgets he has pulled from his "forth-dimensional pocket" over the years. MOFA also appointed three female models as "Ambassadors of Cute" in 2009 to embody icons of fashion—schoolgirl in uniform, Lolita, and Harajuku teenager in a case where life imitating art or art life is at its fuzziest.

The distance from loving and emulating anime characters to paying homage to them through pilgrimage remained but a step away. Soon *seichi junrei* or visits to "holy sites" became part of the promotion initiative. Pilgrimage has a double meaning in the context of anime. There are five pilgrimage destinations for otaku culture itself—Akihabara, Nakano Broadway, and Otome Road in Tokyo, Nipponbashi in Osaka, and Osu in Nagoya where whole blocks are devoted to dives and outlets such as Mandarake that stocks over a million second-hand items—anime, video games, toys, and *dojinshi* (amateur manga). But the second meaning of pilgrimage comprises visits to sites depicted in specific anime. For fans of *The Melancholy of Suzumiya Haruhi*, Nishinomiya in Hyogo Prefecture is a pilgrimage site. For fans of the *Sailor Moon* series, Hikawa Jinja is now a destination for pilgrims where they can offer prayer tablets to the magical-girl character in the anime.

The Daily Yomiuri columnist Sakurai Takamasa is actively engaged in "pop culture diplomacy" at international events. At a Japan Pop Culture Festival in Moscow he spoke of anime pilgrimage, not to traditional "sacred places" but to locations featured in popular anime series. He showed photos of actual locations used as models associated with the anime *Evangelion* and *Haruhi Suzumiya* and in reference to his second pilgrimage to locations associated with Haruhi Suzumiya, he wrote: "Visiting a real location that was featured in an animated series makes me feel like I'm standing at the intersection of the two- and three-dimensional worlds. I think this is the charm of such pilgrimages." (4)

Even a word such as *matsuri*, usually meaning a Shinto "festival," has evolved and assumed a new meaning through otaku subculture. No longer associated only with traditional, national, or neighborhood festivals to shrines that celebrate agricultural and lifecycle events, *matsuri* can now refer to any gathering of fans at otaku events such as the three-day Comiket in Tokyo that attracts over half a million visitors twice a year annually. While Japan's native religion of Shinto animism may create a predisposition to accept the so-called inanimate world as inherently alive, only an active exercise in imagination can allow the kinds of bonds formed today with 2D and 3D non-existent persons and generate a passion and lifestyle that attract similar events across Asia, Europe, and all the way to Baltimore.

Practical Information

Kaiyodo Figure Museum
13-31 Motohamacho
Nagahama-shi, Shiga 526-0059
Tel: 0749) 68-1680
www.ryuyukan.net

Mandarake Grand Chaos
2-9-22 Nishi-Shinsaibashi
Chuo-ku, Osaka 542-0086
Tel: (06) 6212-0771
www.mandarake.co.jp/shop/index_gcs.html

Mandarake
9-28 Doyamacho
Kita-ku, Osaka 530-0027
Tel: (06) 6363-7777
www.mandarake.co.jp/shop/index_osk.html

Osaka Gundam's by Joshin
4-10-1 Nihonbashi
Naniwa-ku, Osaka 556-0005
Tel: (06) 6648-1411
www.joshin.co.jp

Notes

1 Osmond, Andrew. *Satoshi Kon The Illusionist*. Stone Bridge Press, Berkeley, CA, 2009 (p. 22).

2 Katayama, Lisa. "Love in 2-D," *New York Times Magazine*. July 21, 2009. www.nytimes.com/2009/07/26/magazine/26FOB-2DLove-t.html?pagewanted=all&_r=0. Retrieved December 30, 2012.

3 Galbraith, Patrick W. *The Otaku Encyclopedia: An Insider's Guide to the Subculture of Cool Japan*. Kodansha International, Tokyo, 2009 (p. 176).

4 Sakurai Takamasa. "Looking East/Making the Otaku Pilgrimage," *The Daily Yomiuri*. May 13, 2011. http://www.yomiuri.co.jp/dy/features/arts/T110506004050.htm Retrieved January 1, 2013.

References

Condry, Ian. "Love Revolution: Anime, Masculinity, and the Future," *Recreating Japanese Men*. Eds, Sabine Fruhstuck and Anne Walthall. University of California Press, Berkeley, CA, 2011 (pp. 262-283).

Ikuda Yuka. "The Return of the DTM Boom! The Anonymous Talent 'Hatsune Miku'" 1/2 (DTM Buumu Sairai!? Hatsune Miku ga "Horiokosu" Nanashi Miku' *IT Media News*. Sept. 28, 2007. www.itmedia.co.jp/news/articles/0709/28/news066.html Retrieved December 30, 2012.

Miller, Laura. "Cute Masquerade and the Pimping of Japan," *International Journal of Japanese Sociology*. No. 20, Nov. 2011. Murakami Takashi. *Little Boy: The Arts of Japan's Exploding Subculture*. Yale University Press, New Haven, CT, 2005.

CHAPTER 21

Cosplay
Try On Your Alternate Self

C OSPLAY IS A PERFORMANCE ART ENGAGED in by fans who seek to get in touch with a specific character from anime, manga, or video games by dressing up as, say, the human girl "San" who lives with wolves in Miyazaki Hayao's historical fantasy—*Princess Mononoke* (1997). The costuming and reenactment require a precise and detailed knowledge of the character in order to mimic her mannerisms, body language, and the unique way she drapes her pelt cape and wears her hooded half-mask and canine-necklace. Though any character is grist for this grown-up play, cosplayers generally opt for the one with whom they feel a sense of identification, or who provides a vehicle for their creativity, or a template for what they strive to become consciously or subliminally.

Derived from an amalgam of "costume" and "play," the latter word captures the spirit of these off-the-stage carnivalesque role-playing events. Held at massive comic conventions, in clubs, or designated urban streets, much of the fun for cosplayers lies in the encounter with fellow anime enthusiasts who embody their own favorite avatars and will most likely recognize yours. Besides the pleasant shock of character recognition, cosplay creates a safe "space" in which people can put aside their everyday selves and interact with each other within the novel roles they choose to inhabit. In Japan, this imaginative and indirect form of communication through alternate selves aligns with a basic otaku ethos in which personal lives are sublimated in favor of passionate social exchanges about mutual interests and hobbies.

Cosplaying represents a qualitative shift from the role of passive consumer of culture (watching anime) to that of a producer (cosplaying). A fan is convincing in so far as watching anime leads to a second order phenomenon—demonstrating one's grasp of a character through the ability to embody it. The majority of cosplayers create their own outfits minus certain generic accessories like green or blue haired wigs or colored contact lenses that are more easily purchased from specialty stores such as Osaka's CosPatio Geestore. But to accept the challenges involved in costume production is integral to the *gestalt* of cosplaying that frequently involves a personal odyssey through various craft worlds—metalworking, sewing, leatherworking, molding, and even electrical wiring. In the end, the costume is not just an object but an emblem of achievement and the material evidence of new skills acquired. This is especially true when the construction involves weapons, armor, or stepping into the shoes of a *mecha* such as Gigantor.

Cosplayers are used to encountering people not just disinterested in their hobby but who actively ridicule them for their indulgence in an expensive and labor-intensive pass time that culminates in such ephemera as an animation-character costume. But for many cosplayers, the production process and its exhibition in public spaces can also involve teamwork through the creation of an ensemble of characters from the same anime or through an exchange of skills. The whole process boosts self-esteem while it bonds cosplayers to each other. For only those who share the hobby can really appreciate the workmanship that others have put into their costumes.

Enjoyment for some resides in temporarily assuming a celebrity persona and being photographed. These iconic photographs are then posted on social networking sites. It is this type of sharing that has allowed cosplaying to move from a Japanese hobby to a global subculture in which Japan remains the definitive mecca. The community of intense fans meets at conventions, and communicates through social networking sites. Japan's largest one for cosplayers—Cure—indexes characters according to the TV, game, manga, anime, or novel in which they are appear or by individual cosplayers who keep photo galleries of themselves in various characters. Swapping ideas is made even easier through cosplay magazines. The Japanese *Dengeki Layers* and *Cosmode* are both popular magazines though only the latter has an online English version. The English magazine *CosplayGen*, with print and online versions, promotes cosplayers, cosplay events, and Japanese fashion to an international audience. CosplayGen includes training opportunities offered by cosplayers around the world such as a wing-construction, hair-spiking, and even chainsaw techniques.

Takahashi Nobuyuki who first coined the term "cosplay" in a 1984 article for the magazine *My Anime* used it to describe the whole-hearted costumed fans he witnessed at the Science Fiction WorldCon in Los Angeles. Though he was describing a particular kind of fandom, masquerades and costuming are hardly new especially when it comes to the deliberate revival of cultural memory. In the U.S., the Society of Creative Anachronism engages in live-action role-playing but these are reenactments of historical periods rather than characters. They emulate the Middle Ages and the Renaissance for self-amusement and the enjoyment of their guests with bouts of armored combat, equestrian feats, and archery. Their fanciful division of the world into nineteen kingdoms creates a sportive atmosphere of teams. Other groups devoted to Civil War reenactments dress in costume and revisit crucial historical eras and events such as battles. But in both cases, embodying specific characters is not the point.

Japan has its own versions of historical recreations. The city of Iga in Mie prefecture, one of the traditional hometowns of ninja, attracts tens of thousands of people yearly to its "Ninja Festa" that begins on April 1 and lasts up to five weeks. Though real ninja no longer exist in Japan, they thrived from the fifteenth to the seventeenth centuries. During the Festa, the town is full of ninja role-players. And just outside of Kyoto, the Uzumasa-Toei Eigamura, a period-drama film studio, celebrates the Uzumasa-Sengoku Festival annually. This festival pays homage to a character—Sengoku Hidehisa (1552-1614)—a Japanese military commander who failed miserably but later redeemed himself. When Miyashita Hideki's manga—*Sengoku*—based on the warrior's life debuted in 2004, it became an instant hit. This sheds some light on the difference between reenactments and cosplay. Cosplay is based on anime and manga that are both living arts. They keep generating new pools of characters even if these are based on historical models such as Sengoku Hidehisa. Cosplay depends on specificity of character and not the reproduction of genres and types.

Robin Rosenberg, a psychologist who researches comics and cosplay wrote in her book—*What's The Matter With Batman?* (2012)—about the lessons that can be learned from the biographies of superheroes. A youthful trauma transformed Bruce Wayne into Batman, and the physical assault on Tony Stark turned him into the hero Iron Man. In an interview with *Pacific Standard*, Rosenberg commented: "Transforming into someone who isn't passive is the goal of most cosplayers...If someone can get out his 'shy self' by dressing up as Batman, then it's possible to find the same confidence during a job interview."

Cosplayers gather at parks, nightclubs, cafes, amusement parks, but the most powerful magnet is still the Comiket held in winter and summer in Tokyo. This convention is primarily a bazaar for *doujinshi*, a transgressive genre of fanzine that places known characters in unfamiliar situations. But for hardcore fans, cosplay may move from the realm of fun, self-exploration, and skill acquisition into the arena of competitive sports. The World Cosplay Summit (WCS) held in Nagoya since 2003 is an international tournament for cosplayers whose costumes must be handmade and their characters derive from Japanese anime only. With contestants from twenty countries competing in 2012, perhaps before long it will no longer be appropriate to call cosplay a "subculture."

Practical Information

Cosplay Bar Kyoto (Henshin bar)
Bar Ichijo
Foagura shitsu 2 Fl
Asahi Kaikan (southeast)
Ebisumachi 534-34
Kawaramachi-dori, 3-jo-agaru
Nakagyo-ku, Kyoto 604-8005
http://barichijo.web.fc2.com/

Uzumasa-Sengoku Matsuri
Toei Uzumasa Eigamura Kyoto
10 Uzumasa Higashi-hachiokacho
Ukyo-ku, Kyoto 616-8586
Tel: (075) 864-7716
www.toei-eigamura.com/?c=2

CosPatio Geestore Osaka
7-7 Namba Sennichimae
Chuo-ku, Osaka 542-0075
Tel: 06-6630-7655
www.cospa.com/special/shoplist/list/osaka.html

Iga Ueno Ninja Festa
Iga Shiyakusho
116 Ueno Marunouchi
Iga-shi, Mie 518-8501
Tel: (0595) 22-9611
www.city.iga.lg.jp

Reference

Ackerman, Spencer. "Comic Con on the Couch: Analyzing Super-heroes," *Pacific Standard*. May 3, 2012. www.psmag.com/culture/comic-on-th-couch-psychoanalyzing-superheroes-40550/. Retrieved 1/9/13.

PART VI
RELIGION

CHAPTER 22

Buddhist Micro-Temples

WITH MORE THAN 1,600 BUDDHIST TEMPLES, 11 of which are registered as UNESCO World Heritage sites, Kyoto is a mecca for pilgrims and tourists alike. Yet the must-see status of prestigious temples such as Ginkakuji and Kinkakuji has left many of the city's smaller gems virtually unknown to the public. Kyoto is home to hundreds of small temples that are not museums of Buddhism and do not charge entrance fees, but rather exist as living temples. At their best, small temples serve as vibrant nodes of community life. Besides services for ancestors, funerals, and counseling for the *danka*, or congregation of contributing households, that sustains them, some of these small temples are actively involved in both civic affairs and the contemporary artistic life of the city.

Take Honenin temple, for example, named after the priest Honen Shonin (1133-1212), who broke away from the austere orientation of medieval Buddhism on Mt. Hiei straddling Kyoto and Shiga prefectures to make the faith accessible to common people. This temple stands on the site where Honen and his two disciples, Anraku and Juren, erected an image of Amida Buddha, to whom they performed daily services. By the beginning of the 20th century, Honenin had become a family-run temple, and after World War II it became an independent religious corporation distinct from the Jodoshu sect from which it originated.

In recent years, the temple established the nearby Mori no Senta (Friends of the Forest Center), which is devoted to the study and preservation of nature. Guest speakers there have delivered lessons on topics from mushroom behavior to bear hunting. The center, set in the mountains of Kyoto's Sakyo Ward, also offers guided nature hikes up the 466-meter Mt. Daimonji. At the end of the summer Bon Festival, the character "*dai*," meaning "great," is depicted in fire on the mountainside. It is believed the fire's light can guide ancestor's back to the spirit world. The broad path up the mountain (also a favorite of joggers) offers spectacular views of Kyoto, and a pleasant clearing with log benches for a rest before the hike down. Honenin temple's art gallery, housed in the Kodo lecture hall, hosts weekly exhibitions and the main hall holds dozens of concerts throughout the year.

All this activity might give the impression of a rupture in Buddhist tranquility, but the temple compound—with its raked-gravel

platforms that change with the seasons—maintains the peaceful allure that touched novelist Junichiro Tanizaki (1886-1965). He asked to be buried at Honenin temple, and his grave can be found in the cemetery there. Two main factors are responsible for Honenin temple's success: Shinsho Kajita, the renaissance man who is its head priest, and the members of the *danka*, who are attracted by the way Kajita weaves Buddhism, environmentalism, and art into a unified vision.

A 10-minute walk from Honenin temple is Anrakuji, another family-run living temple that has a compelling but tragic history. The priest Honen had Anrakuji built to honor Anraku and Juren, the chief disciples who perpetuated his teachings of salvation for all. The disciples' charisma attracted two princesses in the court of Emperor Gotoba (1180-1239). The two women left the palace to become nuns, and rumors that circulated about the foursome enraged the emperor, who had Honen exiled and his two disciples beheaded. The two nuns, Matsumushi and Suzumushi, took their own lives. The graves of all four are not far from Café Momiji, a restaurant and event space that the temple opened in 2010 with a glamorous flamenco performance.

Anrakuji temple, headed by the 33rd generation priest Shojun Ito, also sponsors exhibitions in its nearby Gallery Hana-iro, working closely with nonprofit organizations on projects that foster social justice. And on the 25th of each month, Anrakuji temple sponsors a market for locally produced vegetables or *Kyo-yasai.*

Anrakuji and Honenin temples are both located just off Tetsugaku no Michi (Philosopher's Path), a 1.8 kilometer tree-lined promenade along Lake Biwa Canal that has Ginkakuji temple at one end and Nanzenji temple at the other. You can stop in for light refreshments at Café Terrazza, located between Anrakuji and Honenin temples on the mountainside of the canal. It's popular for its shady veranda seating and dog-friendly policy. As the days get cooler, a heartier meal can be found next door at Kisaki Yudofu restaurant. The tables are equipped with stoves for nabe hotpot dishes with vegetables and either meat or tofu in rich broth.

Not all small temples thrive as easily as Honenin and Anrakuji. Yasuo Sakakibara took over his family's Jodoshu temple in the Nishijin district of Kyoto after his father's death 40 years ago. Although Sakakibara was a full-time professor of economics at Christian-run Doshisha University at the time, he felt his duty as a son required that he not abandon the temple's congregation of 100 families.

Over time, many of the temple's followers had moved away, some to the suburbs of Kyoto and some as far away as Osaka and Tokyo. The temple had become a place where a person could not possibly make a living solely as a priest. His father had survived as a jack-of-all-trades—cleaner, gardener, repairman and priest— but Sakakibara had to hire different people for each of these roles, continuing only the spiritual duties himself. He also kept teaching as a tenured university professor.

In the summer, he would visit all the homes of the *danka* to pray at the ancestral tablets of their Buddhist altars, and he would conduct six to eight funerals a year. "What happened was a cross-subsidization between religions," he said. "I worked at a Christian university to get money to support a Buddhist temple." After working two full-time jobs for 25 years, Sakakibara was exhausted, but he had no sons and his daughters had no interest in the temple or in marrying temple priests. Eventually, Sakakibara sought a successor from outside his family, trained him, and retired from the temple.

Large Kyoto temples, such as Chionin temple—the head temple of Jodoshu Buddhism—have no *danka* and are run like large companies. The 150 priests who work at Chionin receive a salary from the temple. The majority of the salaried priests have their own small temples elsewhere, but the support of their *danka* alone is not enough for their survival. They use their Chionin salaries to subsidize their own small temples, much like Sakakibara used his salary from the university to sustain his temple.

The large, prestigious temples of Kyoto will always draw crowds, but the priests at the many small temples have to hone their entrepreneurial instincts and find ways to connect to the modern world in Buddhist terms. These small, innovative and unique temples are well worth discovering and seem the leaven of Japanese Buddhism today.

Practical Information

Honenin temple
30 Shishigatani Goshonodancho
Sakyo-ku, Kyoto 606-8422
Tel: (075) 771-2420
www.honen-in.jp
(Temple interior is open to public in 1-7 in November & April).

Friends of the Forest Center
Shishigatani Goshonodancho
Sakyo-ku, Kyoto 606-8422
Tel: (075) 752-4582
www4.ocn.ne.jp/~moricent

Anrakuji temple
21 Shishigatani Goshonodancho,
Sakyo-ku, Kyoto 606-8422
(075) 771-5360
http://anrakuji-kyoto.com

Café Terrazza
72 Shishigatani, Honenincho
Sakyo-ku, Kyoto 606-8421
(075) 751-7931
http://www.cafeterrazza.com

Kisaki Yudofu (Tofu Hotpots)
173-19 Minamidacho Jodoji
Sakyo-ku, Kyoto 606-8403
(075) 751-7406

Hakusasonso Villa (Kaiseki cuisine)
37 Ishibashicho Jodoji
Sakyo-ku, Kyoto 606-8406
Tel: 075) 751-0446
www.hakusasonso.jp

CHAPTER 23

Questing for Connection
Novel and Ancient Pilgrimage

ABOUT FIVE WEEKS AFTER NAOTO KAN stepped down as prime minister in August, he resumed his pilgrimage to the Shikoku region's 88 main temples, which he began back in 2004 with a shaven head. This marked his sixth journey in a pilgrimage done in sections over an eight-year period along the 1,400-kilometer route. His lone figure—a pilgrim's staff in hand and wearing a conical sedge hat, white trousers and jacket—presented an archetypal image of the pilgrim on a quest for healing an rejuvenation through exposure to objects and places held sacred. Pilgrimages—journeys to holy places traditionally made on foot—are thriving worldwide.

Not only have pilgrim numbers soared on ancient, established routes, but visitors to these places historically affiliated with a specific religious and cultural tradition are increasingly coming from far-flung parts of the world. These "pilgrims" may not even share the religion associated with the pilgrimage they are undertaking. What they seek is to connect with the charisma rather than the dogma of a given faith.

The Camino to Santiago de Compostela (Way of St. James)

that stretches from southern France across the north of Spain—a medieval Catholic pilgrimage in origin—is said to receive 100,000 visitors annually. The Shikoku 88 temple pilgrimage, devoted to the ninth-century Buddhist scholar and saint Kukai (774-835) known posthumously as Kobo Daishi, hosts about 300,000 pilgrims a year in lodgings that circle Shikoku—the island of the Daishi's birth.

More surprising still is the popularity of newly created pilgrimages that aspire in the long run to become traditions. Take the case of the enterprising South Korean journalist, Suh Myung Sook, who completed the 800-kilometer Santiago pilgrimage in 2006, and then decided to create her own version of the Spanish Camino on South Korean turf. The following year, the Jeju Olle—a 367-kilometer route of winding paths through seaside towns on her native Jeju Island—opened with 16 trail routes. In 2011, the Santiago-inspired pilgrimage has received a record high of 200,000 visitors.

Japan is hardly lagging when it come to old or new pilgrimages. The steady increase in both pilgrims and pilgrimages dates back to 1953, when the change in the Road Traffic Law allowed huge chartered buses to begin operation. Improvements in road networks, packaged bus tours, increase in car ownership, a growing economy, and improved bridge infrastructure in the decades that followed, all contributed to the surge in pilgrimages. But this alone would not have been enough to mobilize a population were it not for the galvanizing influence of an NHK TV series on the Shikoku pilgrimage. Broadcast between 1998 and 2000, this program offered just the right blend of the idyllic and the cultural.

Indeed, the transformation of pilgrimage from a wayfaring journey to a motorized experience has blurred the boundary between tourist and pilgrim in recent decades, and created a huge potential for the propagation of pilgrimages of a dramatically new kind. I embarked on one of these—the Kinki 36 Fudo pilgrimage—with the intention of walking the whole route that takes in 36 temples, that keep notable images of Fudo-myoo, the Buddhist

Immovable King of Light.

The majority of the temples on the Fudo pilgrimage belong to either the Shingon or Tendai sects of Buddhism. Twelve are located in Osaka Prefecture, 11 in Kyoto Prefecture, Nara, Shiga and Wakayama prefectures have three temples each, while Hyogo Prefecture has four. Established in 1979 by the late Yoshiharu Shimoyasuba, a devout lay Buddhist with a talent for reviving defunct pilgrimages and creating new ones, the Fudo pilgrimage spans the whole Kansai region.

Fudo is an attractive focus of reverence for a pilgrimage. Typically depicted as a bare-chested man of chubby muscularity, either seated or standing on a pile of stones enveloped within a blazing fire, he represents the beginning of the religious quest, the unfolding of a Buddha-like mind, and fierce compassion. The sword in his right hand cuts through human nonsense, and the coiled rope with weights in his left hand catches those ensnared by their own passions and leads them home. The *goma* or fire ceremony, a central ritual of Shingon, Tendai and Shugendo, invokes Fudo's presence with fire to purify the wishes written by people on wooden sticks that are subsequently fed to the flames.

The Fudo pilgrimage promoted by the Kinki 36 Fudo Pilgrim Association attracts about 10,000 pilgrims a year. Unlike the full regalia expected of a pilgrim who walks Shikoku, this pilgrimage requires no special clothing. That also means that there is no way for the public to immediately recognize the pilgrims and treat them accordingly. *Osettai*—the practice of giving money, food or lodgings to a pilgrim and receiving "merit" as a reward—is a venerable tradition in Japan that has long linked pilgrims to the communities through which they pass.

Because the Fudo pilgrimage spans a whole region and the available guidebooks (in Japanese) offer maps with directions only for transportation by train, bus or car, the walking pilgrim faces various challenges. I often asked resident priests at the temples I visited to draw me a map to the next temple—a request sometimes met with astonishment and a recommendation to

take public transportation, or the kind offer of a lift. Since no designated route exists, but only points to be reached, this pilgrimage took me through industrial Osaka Prefecture, sometimes dangerously close to fast-moving traffic, and through the longest covered shopping arcade in Japan. I crossed over the Kanzakigawa and Yodogawa bridges. I had previously only seen the latter from train windows.

Unlike more established pilgrimages, the pilgrims on this route should also bear in mind that temples are likely to close as early as 4 p.m. and many have no lodgings for pilgrims or guests. This is hardly the Santiago de Compostela pilgrimage with its 24-hour open-door policy for pilgrims. Both the creator and the current promoters of the Fudo pilgrimage envisioned a journey done in sections, whereby the pilgrim visits temples on day trips in one prefecture via public or private transportation. To walk the entire route continuously would otherwise take at least a month and require hotel or hostel bookings in advance.

However the pilgrim chooses to travel, a *nokyo-cho*, or small cloth-covered book with thick blank sheets for collecting ink stamps and calligraphic signatures from each temple, is a worthy investment and can be acquired at Shitennoji—the first temple on the route. Here, too, other religious items are available. With a white kimono handy, it is possible to practice *misogi* or purification under a waterfall when a temple offers this option. After all, Fudo is associated as much with water as with fire.

In the final analysis, a pilgrimage is a temporary rupture from daily routine but eventually the pilgrim must go home and reintegrate the lessons learned, for the return is as important as the journey.

Practical Information

Kinki 36 Fudoson Reijokai
(Kinki 36 Fudo Pilgrimage Association)
7-10-102 Sakaemachi
Kawachinagano, Osaka 586-0032
Tel: (072) 56-2372
www.kinki36fudo.org/

Henro Michi Hozon Kyoroku-kai
(Shikoku Pilgrimage Preservation Association)
5-15 Hibarigaoka
Matsuyama 791-8075
Tel: (089) 951-2506
www.iyohenro.jp

Shitennoji temple
1-11-18 Shitennoji
Tennoji-ku, Osaka 543-0051
Tel: (06) 6771-0066

Chishakuin temple
(Daily goma ceremony)
964 Higashikawaracho, Higashioji 7-jo sagaru
Higashiyama-ku, Kyoto 605-0951
(075) 541-5361
www.chisan.or.jp/sohonzan/

CHAPTER 24

Unplanned Obsolescence
Toilets, Technology, and Utopias

NYONE VISITING JAPAN learns quickly about rudimentary boundaries such as leaving your shoes in the entranceway when you visit someone's home and courteously wearing the house slippers indoors. Should you need to use the toilet, special slippers await you in the bathroom that should never leave that room. Toilets and bathtubs are also rarely found in the same room since they belong to two distinct domains—the clean and the unclean. In the case of the toilet, a dedicated room is the norm. Often miniscule and square, it usually accommodates little more than the latrine itself whether a Japanese squat-toilet or a sit-down Western model.

Over the past century, the toilet has become the site of such extraordinary etiquette, symbolism, and technological finesse that it is worth exploring its evolution. Tanizaki Junichiro lauded the toilet somewhat facetiously in his 1933 essay "In Praise of Shadows" as "a place of spiritual repose." In effect, it was (and perhaps still is) the only room in a Japanese house where a person can be guaranteed any real privacy. In the early twentieth century, Tenko Nishida, the founder of Ittoen (Garden of One Light), a utopian community in Yamashina on the outskirts of Kyoto, introduced a spiritual practice known as *rokuman gyougan* (60,000 prayers) that revolved around ritual toilet cleaning.

Tenko-san, as the founder was fondly known, aspired to visit five homes in Kyoto a day for toilet cleaning, an act he repeated two hundred days a year. Tenko considered asking a stranger for permission to clean his toilet, and the act of cleaning itself, as the most humbling of human activities. Inspired to live a life of humility and repentance, Tenko drew his inspiration from eclectic sources: Christ, Gandhi, Tolstoy, but especially from Zen Buddhism. Over many decades, Kyotoites became accustomed to Ittoen squads descending on the city to offer their services for no compensation other than the privilege to serve and polish one's heart in the process of cleaning the toilet. Marching in long lines carrying buckets and dressed in Buddhist work clothes and bandana, these brigades were picturesque and often photographed as somehow emblematic of Japan and a stop-at-nothing work ethic.

In November 2008, I joined Ittoen for one of their three-day retreats (*kenshukai*) to learn about their philosophy and spiritual practices. Immediately upon arrival, I received my uniform—a dark-blue *samue* or Buddhist trousers with a loose shirt and a headscarf. Tenko's grandson—Takeshi—now served as leader of the dwindling community with its impeccable gardens, functioning schools, and an exquisite temple. My fellow retreatants were all from the cleaning company—Duskin—headquartered in Osaka and founded by the businessman Seiichi Suzuki who had joined Ittoen after being cured of a grave illness. Extremely successful as a pioneer of an American-style franchise system, Duskin eventually expanded into Taiwan, Shanghai and South Korea. Ittoen had actually customized this retreat for Duskin employees and simply allowed me to join them. What Ittoen taught in those days represented the moral cultivation expected of those who work for a company that aspires to unite economics with a particular brand of morality. Given the close ties between Ittoen and Duskin, whether or not my close comrades were exempt from the ¥25,000 fee that I paid for the retreat, I never found out.

The first day we embarked on the *rokuman gyougan*. Sixteen of us were divided into small squads each with its own leader. With a bucket and a cloth we marched in single file to the station where we caught a train into the city. My squad's territory happened to be an old neighborhood adjacent to the Kyoto Imperial Palace. With a map, the squad leader indicated our various street assignments. In three hours we were to reconvene at our starting point. The speech we had memorized in order to recite at each house was formulaic. After a greeting, identification of ourselves as from Ittoen and engaged in spiritual practice, we were to say: "*Obenjo no soji o sasete kudasai*" or "Please let me clean your toilet." It surprised me that Ittoen wanted us to use the crudest word for toilet—*benjo*—where *ben-* can mean either "convenience" or "excrement." Other options might have been softer. *Otearai*, for example, comparable to the English word "lavatory," or the simple *toire*, a transliteration of the English for "toilet" would both have been less blunt. But by now the wording had become a tradition. Our diction completely averted asking a question and sounded more like begging.

Standing at the first doorbell, an integrated intercom system, I made my request. After a short silence a female voice told me that she was in no need of toilet cleaning. At the next, I was able to slide open the front door. An elderly man seated in an upraised tatami-mat room called his daughter who apologized; she just happened to be on her way out the door to a doctor's appointment. At the next house an astonished woman snapped at me, "It's not necessary," and shooed me out with a dismissive hand gesture. I had not managed to get into any house to clean a single toilet and dreaded ringing the next bell. I wondered if my foreign accent or appearance had put people off. Maybe it was some kind of TV prank being pulled on them. Or perhaps for the utopian Ittoen the jig was up and they were no longer as welcome as they imagined. I tried another house but it appeared that no one was home at all. I felt that something was fundamentally wrong about this offer of toilet cleaning. Rather than feeling humbled, I felt that I had been a complete nuisance at each place I visited. I decided to quit and go back to the meeting spot and wait for the other people in my squad to finish up.

The second day we devoted to *roto,* that is, going out again in our squads but offering this time to do any kind of work that might be necessary. Here, was an open offer rather than the incredibly direct entreaty: Please let me clean your toilet. The second day's approach resembled the traditional practice of *takuhatsu* when Buddhist monks and nuns go into the streets with a begging bowl for their meals and receive whatever people offer them with gratitude. After a quick surveillance of my squad's neighborhood, I headed directly for a traditional-looking restaurant, slid open the front door and asked the owner how I might assist them that day. The kindly woman gave me a rake and sent me to the garden out back where I happily raked tiny maple leaves until another woman from my squad appeared. Would I lose my plum job now and have to start ringing doorbells again? We ended up dividing the work and eventually both of us were invited inside for lunch. We returned to Ittoen together. It was a happy day.

That evening when all of us gathered to review the experiences of the two days, I learned that only one of the men in our squad had received the opportunity to clean three toilets the first day but he appeared to be the exception. Some of us had a total score of zero. I felt convinced then that the offer to clean toilets was a complete anachronism. Even worse, it was self-centered to expect others to indulge us by letting us clean their toilets just because it happened to be *our* spiritual practice.

Tenko had begun the *rokuman gyougan* practice as an opportunity to help expiate the evils of the world by humbling himself to do the most menial labor imaginable at that time. It was an era when toilets were quite primitive in Japan and probably also quite messy and smelly places to visit. But by 2008 no one wanted or probably even needed their toilets cleaned anymore. We were left with a religious ritual—toilet cleaning—sustained by a foundational myth backed by a utopian commune.

To put this situation in better perspective, toilets used to be located outside the house in Japan. In order to reach them people wore special shoes that would inevitably get dirty. Though the toilet has moved indoors in modern times, the bathroom is still marked as unclean (an outside place) and therefore entering that room requires special footwear. Some of the earliest toilets in Japan from the Nara period (AD 710-784) were built over streams. People used a wooden scraper called a chuugi in lieu of toilet paper that did not come into use until the Edo period (1603-1868). Though depending on the geography of the home, scrapers, leaves, and even seaweed were typical wiping utensils.

Pit latrines have been the most common toilets in Japan throughout the country's history. They were easier to build and maintain than those made of tree branches and placed over flowing streams. In addition, human waste was an important source of fertilizer in an agricultural country where people were largely vegetarian and pescetarian and lacked the manure from livestock raised for food. In 1884, Japan built its first sewage system though it was limited in scope to Tokyo's Kanda district. In most of the country, up until about 1900, brokers or their middlemen carted off human waste generated in the cities and towns to sell to farmers in the countryside. Not until after World War II, and prolonged contact with U.S. Occupation officials who frowned on the use of night soil and promoted chemical fertilizers, did the practice gradually dwindle. This same Japan-U.S. contact influenced the shift from the squat toilet that dominated the industry until 1976 when Western-style toilet began to become more common.

Today Japan possesses the most sophisticated toilets on the planet, along with an elaborate etiquette surrounding defecation. The world's largest sanitary equipment company—Toto Ltd.—is also the country's leading toilet maker. Toto revolutionized the bathroom experience in 1980 with the introduction of its Washlet, a toilet with an integrated bidet. On one side of this Western-style toilet is a computerized control panel with a selection of features.

Among them, a nozzle that emerges from under the seat to squirt jets of warm water whose pressure and temperature may be changed from the panel. After the bottom cleaning, an air dryer blows warm air. For the cold weather, the toilet seat can be heated. Some models even have cool air emission for summer. The Washlet does a pristine job and has even eliminated the need for toilet paper.

Though most public toilets, office lavatories, and 70 percent of Japanese households now have Washlet toilets, they cost anywhere from $900 to $5,000. The higher-end models are self-cleaning, include music systems, and automatic flushing with a deodorizing emission. In addition, Toto faced a delicate gender-related issue squarely. Japanese women using public restrooms typically flushed the toilet multiple times in order to mask any bodily sounds that embarrassed them. This amounted to gallons of wasted water with every visit to the toilet. Toto's elegant solution—the Sound Princess—amounted to a stand-alone or integrated device with a speaker that mimicked the sound of rushing water. No women's restroom seems complete now without a Sound Princess. But if body noises embarrass, so might foul odors. While Toto offered an external solution, the Takano Co. internalized the problem. They manufactured Etiquette Up, tablets you can swallow that make fragrant the smell of both excrement and body gas.

Technology not only renders previous technologies obsolete—what the car did to the horse-and-buggy or the iPad to print magazines—but inevitably changes the meaning of any practice dependent on it. In a country where toilets can now clean themselves as well as those who sit on them momentarily, any spiritual practice based on a primitive assumption about the toilet is hugely mistaken. Revivals and revisions are always possible. In this case, to revivify the original spirit of the *rokuman gyougan* practice would require a leap outside the parameters of Japan.

According to the World Toilet Organization, 2.6 billion people today are without access to sanitary toilets. As a result, they resort to open defecation that leaves them vulnerable to a host of potentially deadly diseases. To hear the sounds of this malodorous world it is imperative to first admit that there is a Sound Princess in the room and then decommission it.

Practical Information

Ittoen
8 Yanagiyama Shinomiya
Yamashina-ku, Kyoto 607-8025
Tel: (075) 581-3136
www.ittoen.or.jp

CHAPTER 25

The Jewel in The Lotus
The Koyasan Buddhist Monastery

K OYASAN MONASTERY is actually a town of over a hundred individual temples spaced neatly around a central complex on a mountaintop basin 800 meters (about 2625 feet) above sea level. Here geology determined destiny: Two rims of hills, each with eight peaks, surround the smooth-capped central mountain. An untrained eye might miss the significance—the whole arrangement suggests a capacious eight-petaled lotus unfolding in the morning mist. The monastery's founding monk Kukai chose this spot as the site on which to establish his training center for Shingon *mikkyo* or Japanese esoteric Buddhism, the country's main Tantric school (Vajrayana).

Other more magical stories of the monastery's founding in the 9th century circulate constantly. But over the years I have come to feel cautious towards them since the fantastical can be a spiritual red herring and easily lead to unreasonable expectations. These stories are also responsible for Shingon's reputation as a quasi-magical sect of Buddhism. One such tale tells of how Kukai, while still in China learning about Buddhism, threw a three-pronged *vajra,* a ritual implement used during prayer, into the sky and of its landing in the top of a pine tree in faraway Japan. Through the assistance of a mountain deity, a hunter, and a two-headed dog, Kukai found the tree, and on that spot decided to build this monastery for Shingon training.

I came to Koyasan monastery from Hawai'i the year after my father died. It was one of my dreams to enter the monastery though in truth much of my image of monastic life derived from Trappist monasteries I had known in the United States. When it was time for me to leave Honolulu, my teacher's wife traveled together with me on Japan Airlines and later by train and rope-way. Shortly after my arrival at my teacher's affiliate temple, I was given nun's clothes and sent to a barbershop in the town to have my hair cut off. In a community like Koyasan, the experienced barber needs no explanation. He knew to leave three tiny symbolic knobs of hair on my head that would be shaven off at my actual entrance ceremony when I took my vows.

Since that year—2000—I have encountered many people in Europe and the U.S. whose comments about Buddhism continue to surprise me. They commonly eschew the word "religion" and claim that Buddhism is instead a "spirituality" or "a way of life" as if that were somehow superior. I wholeheartedly agree that Buddhism is a way of life but no more or less than Christianity, Judaism, Islam, or Hinduism. What religion is not fundamentally about teaching people how to navigate through the physically and morally perilous world into which we have all been born? The point is that Buddhism also has an elaborate theology with heavens and hells (sorry), complex rituals, and various schools with diverse beliefs concerning something as basic to the Buddhist enterprise as "enlightenment." Not only meditation and yogic exercises are part of the package, but rank and hierarchy also exist along with a basic distinction in Japan at least between scholar-monks and practitioner-monks.

I believe that part of the problem in understanding Buddhism, especially outside of Buddhist countries, is basically a linguistic one. Translations continue to mislead and befuddle us. The most vexing one to me has always been the use of the word "emptiness" (*sunyata*) to describe a breakthrough and illumination into a state of pure potentiality. While in Buddhism, the word is purely positive, in English the word "emptiness" carries such a negative connotation such that who in her right mind would aspire to such a state in the first place? Another problematic term is the word "monastery" itself. After watching Philip Groning's splendid documentary about life in the Grande Chartreuse Monastery in the French Alps—*Into Great Silence* (2005)—I had to conclude that no comparable institution exists in Japan. While in training monks and nuns are temporarily celibate, vegetarian, teetotaler, and required to keep the head shaven. Afterwards, the monk or nun can decide which of these practices to resume without criticism from others.

Japanese monks marry and raise their own families and the whole family provides the labor that sustains a temple economically. Individual monks generally have some kind of job in the secular world such as teaching in primary or a secondary school. Since the temple system is patrilineal, a son will typically take charge of the temple when his father retires or dies whether he has a religious "calling" or not, a situation that has bred cynicism among many Japanese. After all, a monk who in his heart would prefer to be a baseball player or a *manga* artist cannot very well perform the many rituals required in the post with conviction or counsel his flock without the wisdom that comes from a spiritual life. In the case of the ten Japanese women with whom I trained, the majority were daughters of temple monks. A few had brothers unwilling to assume the father's responsibility and had been allowed to pursue their own dreams. These young women had boldly stepped up to the plate in their stead. But in the case of nuns the general social expectation is that they will not marry. In any case, temples headed by nuns are extremely rare.

A few months after my entry at the Nuns Training Center, the summer vacation began and my classmates returned home while I went to my affiliate temple to memorize sutras and *dharani* in the basement shrine where no one could hear my many mistakes. My temple was one of the busiest in town during summer months when visitors seek to escape the sweltering heat and humidity below and immerse themselves on the mountaintop in one of the great centers of Japanese Buddhism. *Shukubo* or lodging at a temple for a few days is very popular among Japanese and increasingly for foreigners since Koyasan became a UNESCO World Heritage Site in 2004. Temples have come to depend on this revenue even though monks may complain heartily that they feel more like waiters than anything else during the peak guest season in the summertime. In the mornings visitors can attend the *goma*, a fire ritual for purification performed daily regardless of guests, and in the evenings they can sample exquisite *shojin ryori* or vegetarian cuisine—vegetables and tofu made of roasted sesame seeds melded together with arrowroot, or Koya tofu, a spongy freeze-dried tofu, added to savory soups.

Shingon attracted me more than any other form of Buddhism because of its approach to enlightenment. The way it emphasized the body as a vehicle of spirituality rather than an impediment was like martial arts training (minus the "martial"). Shingon's core doctrine teaches the possibility of becoming a buddha or an "awakened person" through your body (*sokushin-jobutsu*) in this lifetime with a daily practice that involves the Three Mysteries (*san-mitsu*)—methods to unite your body, speech, and thoughts.

When I look at my textbooks now from my training I am struck by how much they are all elaborate instruction manuals: How to make the hundreds of mudras with the hands, how to handle the objects while conducting a ritual, how to hold the rosary while praying, how to walk into the *mikkyo-dojo* correctly. What is conspicuously missing is any interpretation of these actions. However, learning the behavior or *kata* through observation and experience is the usual way to acquire any art or craft in Japan.

Some people may think these exercises ridiculously elaborate and wonder why they are even necessary. My only answer is that humans are hardwired for survival and our actions are rooted in a profound sense of self-preservation. We protect our own turf, our own families, or our own tribes. Shingon training tries to break through this deep fear and transcend a limited sense of being human by creating a space for greater perspective on that situation. Almost all temples will have two mandalas on facing walls. These represent the Diamond World and the Womb World and are effectively maps of spiritual and psychological terrain meant to assist the practitioner in developing wisdom and compassion respectively. Ideally, the two are integrated since compassion without the wisdom to understand what is truly needed in any situation can be disastrous or simply ineffectual.

Even the simplest gesture such as bringing two hands together in prayer is itself symbolic in Shingon. The right hand represents the Mahavairocana the cosmic Buddha, and the left the human realm. You place the two hands together when you pray.

Practical Information

Koyasan Temple Lodging (Shukubo)
Koyasan Shukubo Temple Lodging Association
Koyasan Sankei-Koh Co.,Ltd.
600 Koyasan, Koya-cho, Ito-gun
Wakayama 648-0211
Tel: (0736) 56-2616
http://eng.shukubo.net

Epilogue
Post 3/11

I REMEMBER THAT EARLY SPRING AFTERNOON in Kyoto vividly. We had finally reached the time of year when sweaters give way to shirts. In just three more weeks the buds on the cherry trees would begin to release their petals in that slow-motion freefall that would transform the riverbanks, canal promenades, and temple grounds into billowy pink paradises. Japanese of all ages and from every prefecture would flood into Kyoto to renew themselves through a ritual immersion in the country's cultural symbol of beauty and evanescence. It would soon be impossible to find even standing room on the city buses for as long as the cherry blossoms bloomed.

Seated in an old machiya-turned-schoolhouse around the corner from Mibudera temple, my Japanese teacher and I were poring over a passage in old Japanese when at around 2:46 p.m. the sliding panel doors began to clatter in their grooves and the white board on the wall appeared strangely a-kilter. In an instant, one of the teachers from the second floor came rushing down the narrow near-vertical staircase, shouting: "Earthquake, earthquake!" Quakes are rare enough in Kyoto that we were momentarily at a loss: Should we take cover or dash outside? Before committing to either, the old house had stopped shuttering and an awesome silence fell over us. Nothing had broken, not even a pencil had rolled off a table where we were in the southwest part of the city. Perhaps the machiya's old and creaky condition had only exacerbated the impact of a minor temblor. Or if the quake had been major, the epicenter was definitely distant from Kyoto.

Some five hundred miles away off the northeastern coast of Honshu two tectonic plates on the seafloor had collided at that moment and caused an undersea earthquake larger than any in Japan's recorded history. It lasted only six minutes but the tremendous force was enough to move Honshu, the main island of Japan, eight feet to the east. Within minutes after that 9.0-magnitude jolt, came the tsunami, a series of colossal waves from the Pacific Ocean, rolling relentlessly to shore. The waters uprooted trees, flicked cars into somersaults, smashed fishing vessels to smithereens, buckled causeways, swallowed buildings, and washed entire towns off the face of the earth.

This tsunami was also one of the largest ever recorded, and topped 120 ft. in some areas, with "wave trains" that lasted for two days and reached as far as Chile before the ocean resumed its calm. Closer to its source, along the Tohoku coastline, the tsunami had crashed through the Fukushima Dai-ichi nuclear power plant's defense system—first by sweeping over a sea wall built to withstand a maximum 18-foot tsunami, not the 45-foot one that actually hit—and then by inundating the nuclear facility already shaken by a record-breaking earthquake. Though the sensors detecting the quake switched the plant's three working reactors into shutdown mode forty minutes before the tsunami's arrival, the wave swamped the twelve backup diesel generators located in non-waterproofed buildings and the pumps that served as a cooling system to dump the reactor's waste heat into the ocean. All three reactors suffered meltdowns, and one after another, over a period of days, blew up and released radioactive material into the atmosphere well beyond what became the 12-mile evacuation zone. Worse than the Three Mile Island accident that killed no one and released little radioactivity, it was certainly the world's worst nuclear catastrophe since Chernobyl in 1986.

The triple disaster on this day—March 11, 2011—referred to in Japan as "3/11", will perhaps be remembered as a turning point in modern Japanese history when the people's trust in government officials and power companies lay shattered amidst the rest of the rubble. The earthquake and tsunami claimed the lives of more than 19,000 people, injured over 6,000, and made 334,786 more homeless. Besides the staggering human toll, the damage to property is probably inestimable though the World Bank offered the figure of $235 billion. More than 100,000 buildings were also damaged or destroyed, farmlands were rendered useless for years to come on account of the quantity of salt deposited inland by the tsunami, or contaminated by radioactive particles. In their wake, the earthquake and tsunami generated some 20 million tons of debris, some of it toxic, in the three prefectures most affected— Iwate, Miyagi, and Fukushima—though much of it drifted out to sea or sank to the ocean floor. Nevertheless, clearing the debris scattered across the Tohoku coast became a priority in the reconstruction efforts, yet at the same time a highly contentious issue due to the fear of radioactive contamination. Eight months after the disaster Tokyo became the first territory outside the stricken prefectures to accept trainloads of debris for burning and disposal. Although Osaka agreed to accept 36,000 tons, even as recently as January 2013, local opposition has remained strong for fear of radioactive ash that might be released into the air.

The fear of radioactive fallout strikes deep in the heart of Japan, the only nation to have suffered the gruesome effects from nuclear bombs dropped over Hiroshima and Nagasaki at the close of the Pacific War. The stigmatization of survivors exposed to radiation or *hibakusha* has been an ongoing theme in journalistic and artistic works ever since. Ibuse Masuji's novel *Black Rain* comes immediately to mind (rendered masterfully into film by Imamura Shohei), as does the iconic form the fear assumed in the sci-fi figure of Godzilla, the mutant monster with atomic breath, created in 1954. I glimpsed the fear from my own neighborhood in Kyoto where I knew of few people in the aftermath of the nuclear accident in Fukushima who were willing to buy produce that came from anywhere up north, even the usual apples from Aomori far from the nuclear zone, or dairy products from the northernmost island of Hokkaido. Friends and neighbors constantly remarked that we were so lucky to be in Kansai and linked to the southern food chain receiving our produce from the islands of Kyushu and Shikoku rather than northern Honshu that supplied Tokyo.

The Fukushima Dai-ichi nuclear power plant is but one of Japan's fifty-four nuclear reactors built in an era when nuclear energy appeared to be the way to a clean-energy future and the myth of its safety widely promulgated by a powerful pronuclear lobby that includes the Ministry of Economy, Trade, and Industry (METI). In retrospect, this policy orientation seems quite extraordinary since Japan is one of the most earthquake prone archipelagos in the world. Though the earthquake and tsunami were the natural calamities of March 11, the manmade dimensions of the disaster came into ever sharper focus as weeks turned into months and now already two years have passed.

The first of Fukushima's six reactors was commissioned in 1971, although they were all designed in the mid-sixties. The Tokyo Electric Power Company (TEPCO), in charge of the construction and maintenance of the plant, built the plant on a hill, lowering its incline by 65 feet so that the reactors could be on bedrock and thereby improve their resilience to earthquakes. However, in terms of tsunami, this made the plant far more vulnerable. According to scientists who had analyzed Japan's history of tsunami, mega-waves had hit the region at intervals of 800 to 1,100 years for the past 3,000. Since the last huge tsunami had struck 1,100 years ago, this scientific team from Tohoku University had warned of the high probability of another such wave in the near future in an article published in the Japanese *Journal of Natural Disaster Science* in 2001. Their warning went unheeded. Even aside from that relatively recent warning, in the mid-1960s when engineers designed the plant, records of tsunami of 124 feet hitting the Pacific coast were available, yet TEPCO based its calculations on waves in 1960 generated by a 9.5 quake across the Pacific Ocean in Chile.

What became clear in the aftermath is that this nuclear accident could have been avoided. Despite known geological hazards, TEPCO had no disaster management plan in place either for its workers at the plant or the communities living nearby. Ultimately, 150,000 people had to be evacuated in response to the meltdowns at the Fukushima plant. To avoid panic, both TEPCO and the Japanese government played down the risks by suppressing information about the movement of the radioactive plume. This negligence resulted in some cases in the evacuation of people from lightly to more heavily contaminated areas. On top of this, both the evacuees and those made homeless by the natural disasters did not receive the aid they needed in any timely way although billions of dollars had been donated to Japanese Red Cross and numerous other NGOs. Finally by the summer, and under mounting criticism for his for his blundering lack of leadership in the aftermath of the tsunami and nuclear disaster, Prime Minister Naoto Kan resigned. He picked up his pilgrim's staff and resumed his pilgrimage of the 88 temples of Shikoku.

Japan gets thirty percent of its electricity from nuclear plants. The pre-3/11 plan to increase nuclear power by forty percent by 2017 is unlikely to gain the support it would need. Equally improbable is a radical anti-nuclear stance of the sort Germany assumed in response to the meltdown at Fukushima. Instead, a pervasive lack of trust in authority has augmented the sense that people need to look out for themselves more. That explains the widespread use of dosimeters by private citizens to measure the radiation in food they buy or the areas they visit.

On the positive side, the disaster has generated a keen interest in alternative forms of energy. The use of geothermal holds a huge potential for Japan, a country that sits on about 20,000 MW of geothermal energy, comparable to twenty nuclear reactors. Although not all of that could be cultivated, with careful management, geothermal energy might become a vital local source of energy. Here, Iceland would serve as an excellent example since it produces the same amount of geothermal energy as Japan and uses water from its hot spring to heat houses. Japan is also uniquely situated underneath a zone with one of the highest wind densities in the world. With Flying Electric Generators (FEGs), wind turbines suspended in the sky, energy could be harnessed from trade winds and jet streams. At present, Kyushu University is also developing an Integrated Off-Shore Electric Power Generation Farm that combines solar, wind, tidal, wave, and tension power.

Environmental journalist—Junko Edahiro—has another vision for Japan's future. She has written and lectured passionately on the lessons offered by the earthquake and tsunami. In a TEDx Tokyo talk given in 2011, two months after the disaster, she described Japan's future generation and the new era of her country as one of "De" as in: de-ownership, de-materialization, and de-monitarization. For Edahiro, the triple disaster of 3/11 laid bare for all to see a fundamental loss of resilience in Japanese society. The lifestyle and economic practices have focused for decades on short-term goals based on economic efficiency and convenience. Her program is to shift to a "long-term efficiency" that would necessitate a more profound co-existence with nature, not just for enjoyment but with a knowledge of how to cope with its violent characteristics.

Edahiro advocates the establishment of "buffer zones" for nature. Instead of huge coastal dikes and levees buttressed by a narrow conception that all land space should be for human purposes, Edahiro envisions conscientiously setting aside space for nature. She offers the community of Aneyoshi on the Omoe Pensinsula in Iwate prefecture as an example. Aneyoshi is part of Miyako City that was savaged by the tsunami. However, about 196-feet above sea level and 1,640 feet inland, stands a stone slab set there by the ancestors of the current residents of Aneyoshi. A century ago they had actually experienced devastating earthquakes and tsunami and erected the slab to mark a boundary: Houses should be built at an elevation higher than the marker to ensure safety. Although Miyako was the area worst hit by the tsunami, no one was killed by the tsunami in Aneyoshi. Resilience was an integral part of their land use practices and they respected the distance.

Perhaps only in this light is it possible to appreciate a statement of survivor Satoshi Senzoku in Miyako, Iwate Prefecture who lost his hotel located at the Rikuchu Kaigan National Park: "The sea has been a source of so many benefits for us, so I can't truly resent the tsunami."

References:

Connor, Steve. "The Problem with the Fukushima reactors is their age," *The Independent.* 3/17/11. http://www.independent.co.uk/voices/commentators/steve-connor-the-problem-with-the-fukushima-reactors-is-their-age-2244155.html

Daily Yomiuri. "43,000 move from hard-hit Tohoku prefectures," 1/12/12:3

The Economist. Special Report: Nuclear Energy "The Dream That Failed." 3/10/12: 3-18.

——"Geothermal Energy in Japan: Storm in a Tub." 4/7/12:74.

——"The Fukushima Black Box: A dangerous lack of urgency in drawing lessons from Japan's nuclear disaster. 1/7/12:1-3.

Edahiro Junko. "Resilience and the Steady-State Economy: Japan's Sustainability Lessons from the 2011 Disasters and a Declining Population," *Japan for Sustainability Newsletter.* January 2013: 125. http://www.japanfs.org/en/

Folger, Tim. "The Calm Before the Wave: where and when will the next tsunami hit?" *National Geographic.* 2/12. http://ngm.nationalgeographic.com/2012/02/tsunami/folger-text/1

Johnson, Eric, Ed. *Fresh Currents: Japan's Flow From a Nuclear Past to a Renewable Future.* Kyoto Journal, Heian-Kyo Media, Kyoto, 2012. http://download.freshcurrents.org/FreshCurrents2012-final.pdf

——"Osaka pushes incendiary tsunami debris plan: Move to burn 36,000 tons from Iwate, bury it in bay spooks locals," *Japan Times Online.* 1/12/13.

Marks, Paul. "Can diverse power backups boost nuclear plant safety?" *NewScientist.* 1/16/13. http://www.newscientist.com/article/dn21555-power-backups-to-protect-nuclear-plants-in-a-disaster.html

Yasuda Koji. "Hotels in Tsunami-hit areas struggling," Daily Yomiuri. 6/16/11.

The Tuttle Story

"Books to Span
the East and West"

Many people are surprised to learn that the world's largest publisher of books on Asia had its humble beginnings in the tiny American state of Vermont. The company's founder, Charles E. Tuttle, belonged to a New England family steeped in publishing.

Tuttle's father was a noted antiquarian dealer in Rutland, Vermont. Young Charles honed his knowledge of the trade working in the family bookstore, and later in the rare books section of Columbia University Library. His passion for beautiful books—old and new—never wavered throughout his long career as a bookseller and publisher.

After graduating from Harvard, Tuttle enlisted in the military and in 1945 was sent to Tokyo to work on General Douglas MacArthur's staff. He was tasked with helping to revive the Japanese publishing industry, which had been utterly devastated by the war. After his tour of duty was completed, he left the military, married a talented and beautiful singer, Reiko Chiba, and in 1948 began several successful business ventures.

To his astonishment, Tuttle discovered that postwar Tokyo was actually a book-lover's paradise. He befriended dealers in the Kanda district and began supplying rare Japanese editions to American libraries. He also imported American books to sell to the thousands of GIs stationed in Japan. By 1949, Tuttle's business was thriving, and he opened Tokyo's very first English-language bookstore in the Takashimaya Department Store in Ginza, to great success. Two years later, he began publishing books to fulfill the growing interest of foreigners in all things Asian.

Though a westerner, Tuttle was hugely instrumental in bringing a knowledge of Japan and Asia to a world hungry for information about the East. By the time of his death in 1993, he had published over 6,000 books on Asian culture, history and art—a legacy honored by Emperor Hirohito in 1983 with the "Order of the Sacred Treasure," the highest honor Japan can bestow upon a non-Japanese.

The Tuttle company today maintains an active backlist of some 1,500 titles, many of which have been continuously in print since the 1950s and 1960s—a great testament to Charles Tuttle's skill as a publisher. More than 60 years after its founding, Tuttle Publishing is more active today than at any time in its history, still inspired by Charles Tuttle's core mission—to publish fine books to span the East and West and provide a greater understanding of each.